PATRICK H. PERRINE

Digital Triumph

*An Entrepreneur's Journey Beyond Pixels to Inspire
Global and Distributed Teams*

"The question isn't who is going to let me; it's who is going to stop me."

— AYN RAND

Contents

Preface

Welcome to the digital frontier, where the rules of leadership are rewritten amidst the backdrop of a global and interconnected workspace. 'Digital Triumph' marks a pivotal third chapter in the 'Be A Unicorn: The New Entrepreneur's Ultimate Guide to Success' series, meticulously crafted to guide you through the digital dimensions of leadership and teamwork, as heralded in Step 3 of 'Unicorn Rising: Spearheading in the Digital Realm: Steering Through Distributed and Global Teams.'

As we navigate the seas of the 21st century, the shift towards distributed teams presents a dual challenge and opportunity for today's leaders. 'Digital Triumph' builds upon the insights from 'Unicorn Rising,' offering a blend of visionary leadership principles and practical strategies tailored for the digital age. This volume serves as a comprehensive workbook, featuring actionable advice, exercises, and case studies designed to equip you with the tools necessary for fostering a culture of innovation, resilience, and inclusivity within your digital teams.

Drawing from a wealth of experiences from those who have mastered the art of digital leadership, 'Digital Triumph' invites you to explore the realms of remote collaboration, digital workforce dynamics, and the essence of virtual leadership. It is crafted for entrepreneurs who view the digital landscape as a boundless opportunity for growth, innovation, and connection.

As you delve into this guide, remember that the journey to mastering digital and distributed leadership is an ongoing adventure. It demands a commitment to evolve, a readiness to face new challenges, and an unwavering belief in the transformative power of technology and human ingenuity. 'Digital Triumph' is not merely a guide; it's a testament to the incredible potential that awaits when you lead with foresight, empathy, and a deep commitment to uniting teams across the digital divide.

Thank you for embarking on this journey with 'Digital Triumph.' Together, we will unlock the secrets to thriving in the digital era, embracing the challenges, and celebrating the victories that lie ahead. Let's pave the way for a future where digital leadership and global collaboration drive unparalleled success.

Be A Unicorn: The New Entrepreneur's Ultimate Guide To Success

Dream It, Build It:
An Aspirational Odyssey Through
Entrepreneurship in Ten Inspiring Volumes.

Volume Three

DIGITAL TRIUMPH
An Entrepreneur's Journey Beyond Pixels to
Inspire Global and Distributed Teams

1

The Digital Age and the Evolution of Work

"Change is the law of life. And those who look only to the past or present are certain to miss the future."
— *John F. Kennedy*

As the dawn of the 21st century broke, so did the emergence of the digital age, a period marking a radical shift in the way we perceive and engage with work. The traditional office, once the cornerstone of professional life, has been gradually replaced by the virtual workspace, enabled by rapid advancements in technology and communication. This chapter embarks on an exploration of this monumental shift, examining how it has dismantled age-old paradigms and introduced a new era of flexibility, creativity, and global interconnectedness.

The rise of remote work and distributed teams has not only redefined the concept of workplace but also reimagined the structure of work itself. Enabled by the digital revolution, employees and entrepreneurs alike now navigate a landscape where the lines between work and life blur, offering unprecedented opportunities for balance, autonomy, and collaboration across continents.

Yet, this shift brings with it a set of challenges as diverse and complex as the opportunities it presents. From the nuances of managing a globally dispersed team to fostering a cohesive company culture in a digital realm, the evolution of work in the digital age demands a new set of skills, mindsets, and strategies. This chapter delves into both the transformative impact and the hurdles of this digital renaissance, setting the stage for a deep dive into the future of work.

As we delve deeper into the digital age, we uncover the layers of its impact on work. The shift to remote work has democratized opportunities, allowing talent from every corner of the globe to contribute to projects and initiatives previously beyond reach. This global talent pool has led to the rise of distributed and global teams, each member bringing unique insights, cultural perspectives, and skills.

However, the management of such teams requires a nuanced approach to communication, trust-building, and collaboration. The digital tools that enable remote work also necessitate a new understanding of leadership — one that embraces flexibility, autonomy, and the digital savvy to connect teams across time zones and cultural divides.

Opening Anecdote: The Automattic Approach

Before Automattic became synonymous with remote work's success, it was just a fledgling startup with an unconventional idea: building a global company without a physical office. Its founder, Matt Mullenweg, envisioned a world where work could be done from anywhere, harnessing the power of the internet to collaborate, innovate, and build. Today, Automattic stands as a beacon of remote work's potential, with employees across over 70 countries, proving that digital tools can not only replace the traditional office but also enhance productivity, creativity, and work-life balance.

> **Quick Thought:**
> *Embracing the digital work revolution is not about abandoning all traditional practices but about adapting them to harness the full potential of global connectivity and technological advancements.*

Entrepreneurship in Action: Key Ingredients

- **Adaptive Leadership:** The digital age demands leaders who can navigate the complexities of remote teams, leveraging technology to foster communication, culture, and collaboration.
- **Technological Proficiency:** Mastery of digital tools is essential, not just for productivity but for creating an environment where remote work thrives.
- **Cultural Intelligence:** Understanding and embracing cultural differences is key to building strong, cohesive teams in a globally connected workspace.

Case Study: GitLab's Pioneering Approach to Remote Innovation

Background: GitLab, a global leader in the development of software for source code management and CI/CD (Continuous Integration/Continuous Deployment), has set the gold standard for remote work long before it became a global necessity. Founded in 2011, GitLab's journey from a fully remote startup to a powerhouse in the software industry underscores the transformative power of embracing innovation and continuous learning within a distributed team.

Fostering a Culture of Continuous Innovation: From its inception, GitLab has operated on the principle that great ideas and innovation can come from anywhere, not just from within the confines of a physical office. This belief has been embedded into their operational framework through practices such as asynchronous communication, transparent documentation, and an open-source collaboration model that invites contributions from GitLab team members and the wider community alike. This approach has not only accelerated product development and improvement but has also cultivated a culture where continuous learning and innovation are part of the daily workflow.

Leveraging Technology to Enhance Collaboration: GitLab's utilization of its own platform alongside other digital tools exemplifies how technology can bridge the gap between remote team members scattered across the globe. By adopting tools that facilitate seamless collaboration and communication, GitLab has ensured that its distributed team remains united in their goals, with a shared commitment to pushing the boundaries of what is possible in software development.

Empowering Team Members through Learning: Central to GitLab's ethos is the investment in its team's professional growth and development. Recognizing the rapid pace at which the tech industry evolves, GitLab encourages its employees to pursue continuous learning opportunities. This is achieved through a combination of internal resources, like GitLab University, and external courses and certifications, fully supported by the company. This commitment to learning ensures that every team member is not only equipped with the latest skills and knowledge but is also motivated to innovate and contribute to GitLab's success.

Achievements and Impact: The result of GitLab's pioneering approach to remote work, innovation, and learning is evident in its robust product development pipeline, its ability to attract top talent from around the world, and its impressive growth trajectory. GitLab's success story serves as a powerful case study for how remote teams can thrive in an environment that prioritizes flexibility, open communication, and a relentless pursuit of innovation.

GitLab's journey underscores the significant impact of cultivating a remote work culture that embraces innovation and continuous learning. By breaking down geographical barriers and fostering an inclusive environment where every team member can contribute to their fullest potential, GitLab has not only achieved remarkable success but has also redefined what it means to work in the digital age. Their story is a testament to the fact that with the right leadership, tools, and commitment to development, remote teams can drive innovation and set new standards in their industries.

Pro Tip: Embrace flexibility and trust. Remote work thrives in environments where employees are trusted to manage their schedules and workloads, fostering a culture of responsibility and mutual respect.

Exercise: Navigating the Digital Work Transition Workshop

Adapting to Remote Work Dynamics:

- **Digital Collaboration Assessment:** Spend one week exclusively utilizing digital tools for all work-related communications and collaborations. Document both the challenges encountered and the efficiencies gained. This exercise aims to highlight areas for improvement in digital tool usage and strategies to enhance remote collaboration effectiveness.
- **Time Zone Integration Exercise:** Plan and execute a virtual meeting involving team members across different time zones. The goal is to develop an inclusive scheduling approach that considers the diverse time zones of all participants, focusing on maximizing participation while minimizing inconvenience.

Embracing the Digital Leadership Role:

- **Leadership Style Reflection:** Reflect on your current leadership approach and identify aspects that could be better adapted to the digital age. Consider how flexibility, cultural intelligence, and technological proficiency could enhance your effectiveness as a leader. Set a specific goal for development in one of these areas and outline steps for progress.

- **Cultural Intelligence Quiz:** Engage with an online cultural intelligence platform or quiz to assess your current level of cultural awareness and understanding. Based on the results, identify specific actions you can take to improve your ability to lead a culturally diverse team effectively.

Fostering Digital Innovation:

- **Innovation Brainstorming Session:** Organize a virtual brainstorming session with your team to identify innovative approaches to remote work challenges. Encourage the use of digital whiteboarding tools to facilitate idea sharing and collaboration. Summarize the session with actionable steps to implement the best ideas.
- **Remote Work Policy Review:** Examine your current remote work policies and identify areas that could be updated or expanded to better support remote work dynamics. Consider aspects such as communication protocols, digital tool usage, and work-life balance initiatives.

Challenge for You:

Over the next three months, implement a new strategy or tool aimed at enhancing one aspect of your digital work environment. This could involve improving team communication, increasing cultural intelligence, or adopting a new digital tool for collaboration. Monitor the impact of this change on team dynamics and productivity, making adjustments as necessary based on feedback and results.

Concluding Thoughts:

As we close this chapter on the dawn of the digital age and the evolution of work, it's clear that we stand on the brink of a transformative era. The journey into remote work is not merely a shift in location but a profound change in how we connect, innovate, and achieve our collective goals. Entrepreneurs and leaders who navigate this new landscape with flexibility, cultural intelligence, and an embrace of technological tools will not only thrive but also pioneer new ways of working that were once thought impossible. The future of work is here, and it promises a world where distance is no barrier to collaboration, where creativity knows no bounds, and where every individual has the opportunity to contribute to something greater than themselves. Are you ready to seize this moment, to lead with vision and empathy, and to shape a future where work is not just about what we do, but how we bring people together across the digital divide?

2

The Impact of Distributed and Global Teams

"The strength of the team is each individual member.
The strength of each member is the team."
— Phil Jackson

I n the vast expanse of the digital age, the emergence of distributed and global teams stands as a testament to the limitless potential of collaborative work across borders. This chapter ventures into the heart of this paradigm shift, revealing how the digital revolution has dismantled traditional organizational structures to favor a more inclusive, diverse, and flexible work environment. By transcending geographical and cultural barriers, these teams have become pivotal in driving innovation, enhancing productivity, and fostering a global perspective within businesses.

The advantages of embracing distributed and global teams are manifold, offering organizations a competitive edge in the global marketplace. From tapping into a vast reservoir of talent across different time zones to achieving round-the-clock productivity, these teams epitomize the synergy between diversity and creativity. Their formation marks a strategic move towards embracing inclusivity, leveraging a wide array of skills and perspectives to solve complex problems, and innovating in ways previously unimaginable.

However, the path to harnessing the full potential of these teams is fraught with challenges. Differences in time zones, language barriers, and cultural nuances pose significant hurdles to seamless collaboration and communication. This chapter delves into these obstacles, offering insights into overcoming them and laying out strategies for building cohesive, effective teams that thrive on diversity and mutual respect.

The landscape of distributed and global teams is rich with opportunities for innovation and growth. By embracing diverse talents and perspectives, organizations can unlock novel solutions and insights, propelling them towards unprecedented success. Yet, the intricacies of managing such teams demand a nuanced approach to leadership, communication, and cultural sensitivity.

Effective communication stands as the cornerstone of distributed team management, requiring leaders to be adept in leveraging digital tools and fostering an environment of openness and transparency. Building trust and cohesion in a virtual space necessitates intentional efforts, from regular virtual meet-ups to acknowledging and celebrating team achievements.

Opening Anecdote: The Buffer Blueprint

Buffer, a pioneer in social media management, embodies the ethos of distributed teamwork, operating with a fully remote team spread across the globe. Their journey from a conventional startup to a remote work powerhouse illuminates the possibilities and challenges of distributed teams. Buffer's transparent, trust-based culture and strategic use of technology have enabled them to navigate the complexities of remote collaboration, setting a benchmark for companies worldwide.

> *Quick Thought:*
> *The true power of distributed and global teams lies not in their geographical spread but in their ability to function as a unified entity, transcending physical and cultural barriers to achieve common goals.*

Entrepreneurship in Action: Key Ingredients

- **Diversity and Inclusion:** Harnessing the diverse perspectives and experiences of team members to foster innovation and creativity.
- **Effective Communication:** Utilizing digital tools to maintain clear, open channels of communication, ensuring all team members are aligned and engaged.
- **Trust and Transparency:** Building a culture of trust through transparency, mutual respect, and shared values.

Case Study: Soko's Global Artisan Empowerment

Background: Soko, a pioneering social enterprise founded by Gwendolyn Floyd, Ella Peinovich, and Catherine Mahugu, offers a striking example of leadership and innovation in a distributed work environment. Launched with the mission to transform the traditional model of the global supply chain, Soko empowers artisans in developing countries by connecting them directly with the global marketplace through mobile technology.

Championing Cultural Sensitivity and Inclusion: Central to Soko's ethos is a deep respect for the cultural heritage and craftsmanship of its artisan partners. By acknowledging and celebrating the diverse cultural backgrounds of its team members and artisans, Soko has fostered an inclusive environment that transcends geographical boundaries. This approach not only enhances the richness of the product offerings but also strengthens the bonds within the team, promoting a shared commitment to Soko's mission.

Leveraging Technology for Empowerment: At the heart of Soko's operational model is an innovative use of mobile technology that allows artisans to upload and manage their product listings directly from their smartphones. This technology empowers artisans in remote areas, many of whom have limited access to traditional marketplaces, enabling them to participate in the global economy on their terms.

Building Resilience and Adaptability: Soko's distributed team, spanning from Nairobi to San Francisco, embodies the principles of resilience and adaptability. By leveraging digital tools for communication and collaboration, the team navigates the challenges of time zones, language barriers, and cultural differences. Regular virtual meetings, clear communication protocols, and a culture of mutual support ensure that every team member, regardless of location, feels valued and connected.

Driving Innovation through Continuous Learning: Committed to continuous improvement and innovation, Soko encourages its team and artisan partners to engage in ongoing learning and development. Through workshops, training sessions, and collaborative projects, Soko fosters a culture of curiosity and creativity that fuels its mission to redefine ethical fashion and artisan empowerment.

Impact and Legacy: Soko's success illustrates the transformative power of embracing innovation and cultural diversity within distributed and global teams. By building a business model that prioritizes social impact, cultural respect, and technological innovation, Soko has not only achieved commercial success but has also made significant strides in improving the lives of artisans around the world. The company's journey serves as an inspiring case study for how distributed teams can drive change and create value in the digital age.

Soko's approach to managing distributed and global teams highlights the importance of cultural sensitivity, technological empowerment, and a commitment to social impact. Through innovative leadership and a dedication to continuous learning, Soko has navigated the complexities of the digital workplace, emerging as a model for sustainable and inclusive business practices. Their story is a testament to the potential of distributed teams to foster innovation, bridge cultural divides, and make a meaningful difference in the world.

Pro Tip: Prioritize asynchronous communication and documentation. This approach respects the varied schedules of a global team, ensuring everyone can contribute meaningfully regardless of their time zone.

Exercise: Enhancing Distributed Team Dynamics Workshop

Cultural Awareness and Integration:

- **Global Cultural Showcase:** Organize a series of virtual sessions where team members present on their local culture, customs, and how these influence their work practices. This initiative aims to celebrate diversity and foster a deeper understanding among team members.
- **Cultural Sensitivity Quiz:** Create or utilize an existing online quiz to assess and enhance team members' cultural sensitivity. Discuss the results in a team meeting, highlighting the importance of cultural awareness in a global team's success.

Asynchronous Collaboration Mastery:

- **Distributed Brainstorming Challenge:** Launch a week-long asynchronous brainstorming activity using a collaborative online tool. Set a theme related to improving team workflows or solving a common challenge. Encourage participation from all team members, regardless of their time zones, and compile the outcomes for review and implementation.

- **Time Zone Empathy Exercise:** Have team members swap schedules with a colleague in a significantly different time zone for one day. This exercise aims to build empathy and understanding of the scheduling challenges faced by remote team members.

Building Trust and Transparency:

- **Trust Circle Virtual Meetings:** Initiate monthly virtual "trust circles" where team members can share personal achievements or challenges within a supportive environment. The goal is to strengthen interpersonal relationships and build trust within the team.
- **Transparency Log:** Implement a shared digital log where team members can voluntarily record their weekly achievements and learning moments. Encourage the team to review and comment on entries, promoting a culture of openness and mutual support.

Challenge for You:

Identify an area within your distributed team that requires improved cohesion or efficiency. Implement a targeted initiative from the workshop activities over the next three months, focusing on either cultural integration, asynchronous collaboration, or trust-building. Document the strategy, execution, and impact, making adjustments based on team feedback and observed outcomes.

Concluding Thoughts:

As we conclude this exploration into the world of distributed and global teams, it becomes evident that the future of work is not rooted in a place but in people—diverse, dynamic, and dispersed across the globe. The digital age offers us the unparalleled opportunity to harness the collective power of these teams, transcending traditional barriers to unlock innovation, creativity, and productivity on a global scale. By embracing the challenges and leveraging the strengths inherent in this new paradigm, entrepreneurs and leaders can forge pathways to unprecedented success. The journey forward requires resilience, adaptability, and a commitment to fostering an inclusive, communicative, and collaborative work culture. As we venture into this evolving landscape, the potential for growth and transformation is boundless. Are you ready to lead your distributed team with vision, empathy, and strategic insight, charting a course through the complexities of the digital age towards a future bright with possibility?

3

Defining Your Leadership Style in a Digital Context

"Leadership is not about being in charge.
It is about taking care of those in your charge."
— Simon Sinek

The advent of the digital age has catalyzed a paradigm shift in leadership dynamics, compelling leaders to reassess and redefine their approaches to suit the virtual realm. As the fabric of the traditional workplace undergoes a digital transformation, the essence of effective leadership is increasingly characterized by adaptability, empathy, and a commitment to fostering an inclusive, empowered environment. This chapter embarks on a journey to explore the criticality of sculpting a leadership style that resonates with the ethos of digital collaboration, ensuring leaders are equipped to navigate the intricacies of managing distributed and global teams.

The shift from hierarchical to more agile, team-centric leadership models underscores the evolution necessitated by the digital era's demands. In the realm of distributed teams, leadership transcends physical boundaries, requiring a nuanced blend of technology proficiency, emotional intelligence, and a servant leadership ethos. These attributes form the cornerstone of a digital leadership style that champions transparency, fosters collaboration, and cultivates an environment where innovation flourishes.

Identifying and honing one's leadership style within this digital context is not merely an exercise in self-awareness but a strategic imperative for driving team cohesion, productivity, and engagement across distances. Through self-reflection, leveraging strengths, and addressing developmental areas, leaders can craft a personalized approach that aligns with the unique demands of digital-age teams. This chapter guides leaders through the process of adapting their leadership styles, embodying the traits of successful digital leadership, and applying these insights in practical, impactful ways.

In the digital workplace, leaders face the dual challenge of maintaining team cohesion and driving performance without the benefit of physical presence. Embracing servant leadership, where the focus shifts from commanding to supporting, enables leaders to meet these challenges head-on. This style prioritizes the growth and well-being of team members, creating an atmosphere of trust and mutual respect essential for remote teams.

Emotional intelligence emerges as a pivotal leadership competency in the digital context, enabling leaders to connect with their team members authentically and foster a sense of belonging. Through active listening, empathy, and effective conflict resolution, leaders can cultivate a team culture that thrives on collaboration and open communication.

Opening Anecdote: The Zapier Empathy Model

Zapier, a leader in automation software, operates with a fully remote team and champions a leadership style deeply rooted in emotional intelligence. Their emphasis on empathy, understanding, and proactive communication has not only bridged the physical gaps between team members but also fostered a robust, supportive culture. This approach has enabled Zapier to navigate the complexities of digital collaboration effectively, setting a precedent for how leaders can harness emotional intelligence to enhance team dynamics and performance.

> *Quick Thought:*
> *The essence of digital leadership lies in the ability to inspire and influence across screens, transcending physical barriers to create a shared vision and purpose.*

Entrepreneurship in Action: Key Ingredients

- **Empathy and Understanding:** Demonstrating genuine care for team members' well-being and professional growth.
- **Open and Transparent Communication:** Ensuring that all team members feel informed, involved, and valued.
- **Empowerment and Autonomy:** Encouraging innovation and decision-making at all levels, building a culture of trust and accountability.

Case Study: Tala's Visionary Approach to Global Financial Inclusion

Background: Shivani Siroya, the founder and CEO of Tala, embarked on a mission to redefine financial access for underserved populations around the globe. Tala, a fintech startup, leverages mobile technology to provide microloans to individuals in emerging markets without traditional banking access. Siroya's visionary leadership and innovative use of technology have propelled Tala into a leading platform for financial inclusion, demonstrating the profound impact of adaptive leadership in the digital age.

Embracing Cultural Diversity and Inclusion: Central to Tala's success is Siroya's commitment to understanding the unique cultural and economic landscapes of its users. By fostering a team culture that values empathy and inclusivity, Tala has been able to tailor its services to meet the specific needs of diverse populations. This approach not only enhances user experience but also strengthens the team's cohesion and drive towards a common goal of making financial services accessible to all.

Innovative Use of Technology for Empowerment: At the heart of Tala's operations is its proprietary credit-scoring algorithm, which analyzes mobile data to assess creditworthiness. This groundbreaking approach bypasses traditional banking barriers, enabling Tala to extend credit to individuals previously deemed "unbankable." Siroya's leadership in embracing mobile technology illustrates the transformative potential of digital tools in addressing global challenges.

Fostering a Growth Mindset and Continuous Learning: Under Siroya's guidance, Tala cultivates a culture of continuous learning and innovation among its team members. By encouraging experimentation and embracing failures as learning opportunities, Tala remains at the forefront of fintech innovations. Regular training sessions, knowledge-sharing forums, and a supportive environment for personal and professional growth underscore Tala's commitment to its team's development.

Impact and Legacy: Tala's journey under Siroya's leadership exemplifies how embracing innovation and fostering a culture of inclusivity and continuous learning can drive change on a global scale. With millions of users across countries like Kenya, the Philippines, Mexico, and India, Tala has not only provided financial access to those in need but has also contributed to economic empowerment and poverty reduction.

Shivani Siroya's leadership at Tala highlights the critical importance of adapting leadership approaches in the digital context to address global challenges. By leveraging technology for social good, prioritizing cultural sensitivity, and promoting a growth mindset, Tala has set a benchmark for digital-age leadership. Siroya's journey offers invaluable insights into building resilient, innovative, and inclusive teams that can navigate the complexities of the digital world, making a lasting impact on society.

```
Pro Tip: Cultivate a culture of feedback -- both
giving and receiving. It's crucial for continuous
improvement and helps in aligning team efforts with
organizational goals.
```

Exercise: Adaptive Leadership in the Digital Age Workshop

Emotional Intelligence and Empathy Development:

- **Empathy Mapping Session:** Organize an activity where leaders map out potential emotional responses of team members to various scenarios. This exercise aims to deepen leaders' empathy by understanding diverse perspectives and emotional triggers within the team.
- **Emotional Intelligence Self-Assessment:** Utilize an online EI assessment tool to identify strengths and areas for growth in your emotional intelligence. Develop an action plan to enhance your EI skills, focusing on areas such as self-awareness, self-regulation, and empathy.

Transparent and Effective Digital Communication:

- **Digital Communication Audit:** Review your past week's communications, identifying instances where clarity or inclusivity could have been improved. Develop a set of personal guidelines for effective digital communication, including principles for clarity, tone, and inclusiveness.
- **Inclusive Communication Workshop:** Conduct a virtual workshop with your team on inclusive communication practices. Discuss the importance of language, tone, and platforms in ensuring everyone feels heard and respected. Implement a monthly check-in to discuss and evolve these practices.

Fostering Autonomy and Empowerment:

- **Delegation Diagnostics:** Reflect on recent projects or tasks and identify opportunities where delegation could have been implemented more effectively. Create a delegation plan for an upcoming project, specifying tasks, responsible team members, and expected outcomes.
- **Autonomy Action Plan:** Design an action plan to enhance team autonomy, including setting clear expectations, providing resources and support, and establishing feedback loops. Share this plan with your team and solicit their input to ensure alignment and buy-in.

Challenge for You:

Choose one leadership attribute you wish to enhance—empathy, digital communication, or empowerment. Over the next three months, actively apply strategies from this workshop to improve in that area. Document your journey, noting any changes in team dynamics, feedback from team members, and personal reflections. Share your experiences and lessons learned with your team, fostering a culture of continuous leadership development.

Concluding Thoughts:

Embarking on the journey of leadership within the digital realm offers a unique opportunity to redefine the essence of effective guidance and support. This chapter has illuminated the pivotal role that adaptability, empathy, and a commitment to inclusivity play in navigating the complexities of remote team management. The digital age challenges leaders to transcend traditional paradigms, advocating for a leadership style that resonates across virtual spaces, fostering an environment ripe for innovation, collaboration, and mutual respect. By integrating these key principles, you stand at the threshold of transforming not only your leadership approach but also the collective potential and success of your team. Ready to embrace the challenges and opportunities that lie ahead, your journey as a digital-age leader is poised to inspire a new era of connectivity, growth, and transformative leadership.

4

Cultivating a Culture of Trust and Collaboration

"Trust is the glue of life. It's the most essential ingredient in effective communication. It's the foundational principle that holds all relationships."
— Stephen R. Covey

In the intricate tapestry of the digital workplace, the threads of trust and collaboration are interwoven, forming the fabric that binds distributed and global teams together. As the digital age redefines the boundaries of work, the ability of leaders to foster a culture brimming with trust and seamless collaboration becomes paramount. This chapter delves into the nuanced dynamics of nurturing a workplace where trust transcends physical distances, and collaboration becomes the engine of innovation and success.

Trust in remote teams is not merely a foundational element; it's a catalyst that propels teams towards efficiency, unity, and resilience. In the absence of conventional face-to-face interactions, establishing trust becomes both a challenge and an opportunity. It's about creating a virtual environment where transparency, accountability, and mutual respect flourish. This chapter explores practical strategies for leaders to build and sustain trust, laying the groundwork for a culture where collaboration naturally thrives.

Collaboration in the digital realm transcends the simple act of working together; it embodies the spirit of collective intelligence and creative synergy. Yet, fostering this collaborative spirit requires overcoming inherent barriers of distance, time zones, and cultural differences. By highlighting effective communication practices and tools, this chapter guides leaders on how to enhance collaboration, ensuring that every team member feels valued, heard, and connected, regardless of their geographic location.

Building trust in a distributed team starts with transparency and consistent leadership. By setting clear expectations and being accountable, leaders can model the behaviors they wish to see, fostering an atmosphere where trust grows. Virtual team-building activities and informal virtual coffee breaks can also play a pivotal role in strengthening interpersonal relationships.

Effective communication is the linchpin of collaboration in remote settings. Leaders must champion clear, concise, and empathetic communication, employing a variety of tools to bridge the gap between team members. Overcoming communication barriers requires a proactive approach, ensuring inclusivity and understanding across diverse team members.

Opening Anecdote: The InVision Initiative

InVision, a digital product design platform, thrives with a fully remote workforce by embedding trust and collaboration at the heart of its culture. Through initiatives like Design Sprints, InVision demonstrates how distributed teams can collaborate intensely and innovatively. Their commitment to open feedback and creating collaboration opportunities exemplifies how trust and teamwork fuel creativity and propel the company forward in the competitive tech landscape.

> *Quick Thought:*
>   *Cultivating trust and fostering collaboration in remote teams is akin to weaving a strong net—it holds the team together, catching and uplifting every member, enabling them to achieve their collective and individual goals.*

Entrepreneurship in Action: Key Ingredients

- **Transparency and Accountability:** Leaders must be open about decisions and actions, showing consistency in words and deeds.
- **Open Dialogue and Feedback:** Encourage regular, constructive feedback and open channels of communication to build trust and improve team dynamics.
- **Recognition and Empowerment:** Acknowledge individual contributions and empower team members to take initiative and make decisions.

Case Study: 15Five's Culture of Continuous Feedback and Growth

Background: 15Five, a performance management software company, has carved a niche in fostering employee development and creating a culture of trust through continuous feedback. Founded by David Hassell, 15Five has championed the philosophy that regular, honest feedback and open lines of communication are fundamental to personal and professional growth. Their software is designed to facilitate weekly check-ins, objectives and key results (OKRs), and 1-on-1 meetings, thereby bridging the gap between managers and their teams in remote settings.

Leadership Philosophy: David Hassell's leadership style is deeply rooted in the belief that transparency and trust are pivotal to a team's success, especially in a distributed work environment. He advocates for a leadership approach that empowers employees, encourages risk-taking, and supports career development. Hassell's vision for 15Five was to create a tool that not only enhances productivity but also nurtures a supportive culture where feedback drives improvement.

Implementing Change: As 15Five grew, maintaining a culture of trust and collaboration across a distributed team presented a unique set of challenges. Hassell and his team were committed to using their own platform to overcome these hurdles, ensuring that every employee, regardless of their location, felt connected, valued, and understood. They implemented structured feedback mechanisms and regular virtual meetings to foster open dialogue and ensure alignment on company goals.

Cultivating Trust and Collaboration: Under Hassell's

leadership, 15Five has demonstrated that creating a virtual environment where employees feel safe to express their thoughts and ideas is crucial for innovation and team cohesion. By prioritizing regular, structured feedback, 15Five has enabled its team to thrive, with employees feeling more engaged and motivated to contribute to the company's success.

Outcome: The strategies employed by 15Five have not only enhanced their internal team dynamics but also positioned the company as a leader in the employee engagement and performance management space. Their success illustrates the power of a feedback-rich culture in driving employee satisfaction and organizational growth, especially in remote settings.

Legacy and Insights: 15Five's journey underscores the significance of adapting leadership strategies to meet the demands of the digital age. Hassell's approach to fostering open communication, trust, and continuous learning has set a benchmark for how companies can successfully navigate the challenges of distributed work. This case study exemplifies the transformative impact of building a culture where feedback is not just encouraged but is integral to the workflow, ensuring that every team member has the opportunity to grow and succeed.

By integrating their own product into their operational ethos, 15Five has proven that the right tools, when used to support a clear vision of trust and continuous improvement, can significantly enhance team productivity and morale. This case study serves as a blueprint for leaders looking to cultivate a resilient, innovative, and collaborative team culture in a remote work landscape.

```
Pro Tip:
Make regular, intentional efforts to connect with
team members on a personal level. Understanding
personal motivations and challenges can enhance
trust and collaboration.
```

Exercise: Building Trust and Enhancing Collaboration in Virtual Teams

Fostering Trust through Transparency and Accountability:

- **Transparency Action Plan:** Develop a plan that outlines specific actions you will take to increase transparency in your leadership approach. This might include open discussions about team goals, sharing progress on key projects, or transparent decision-making processes.
- **Accountability Partnership:** Pair up team members as accountability partners. Encourage them to set weekly goals and check in with each other on accomplishments and challenges, fostering a culture of mutual accountability and support.

Strengthening Relationships and Empathy:

- **Virtual Empathy Workshop:** Host a workshop focusing on empathy in virtual communications. Incorporate role-playing scenarios to practice understanding and responding to the emotions and perspectives of others, especially in challenging situations.

- **Personal Story Exchange:** Organize a session where team members are encouraged to share stories about their backgrounds, hobbies, or any personal experiences they feel comfortable sharing. This activity aims to deepen connections and understanding among team members, going beyond work-related topics.

Enhancing Collaboration with Practical Exercises:

- **Collaborative Problem-Solving Challenge:** Designate a common challenge or project goal. Divide the team into small groups to brainstorm solutions using a shared digital workspace. Encourage creativity and the sharing of diverse perspectives, followed by a group discussion to refine ideas and develop a unified approach.
- **Feedback and Improvement Loop:** Implement a structured feedback loop where team members can give and receive feedback on collaborative projects. Focus on constructive feedback that enhances team dynamics and project outcomes. Use digital tools to facilitate anonymous feedback if necessary.

Challenge for You:

Select one area of focus—either enhancing trust through transparency and accountability, strengthening empathy and personal connections, or improving collaborative practices. Over the next three months, implement targeted strategies from this workshop aimed at this area. Document the strategies used, observe the changes in team dynamics, and gather feedback from team members on the effectiveness of these approaches. Share your findings and adjustments made based on feedback in a team meeting to foster a continuous cycle of improvement.

Are You Prepared to Foster Trust and Collaboration?

Embarking on the journey to cultivate a culture of trust and collaboration within distributed teams is a transformative endeavor, requiring commitment, empathy, and strategic insight. Are you ready to lead by example and unlock the collaborative potential of your team?

Concluding Thoughts:

In this digital age, the journey towards fostering a culture of trust and collaboration within remote teams marks a significant milestone in the evolution of work. This chapter has laid the groundwork for understanding the crucial elements that drive such a culture, emphasizing the importance of transparency, accountability, and mutual respect. As leaders, the task ahead involves continuously striving to bridge the physical and emotional gaps that distance can create, turning challenges into opportunities for strengthening team bonds. By embracing the strategies and insights shared, you are now better equipped to lead your team into a future where trust and collaboration are not just ideals but the very pillars upon which your team's success is built. The path forward is clear—embrace these principles with conviction, and watch as your team transforms into a more cohesive, innovative, and resilient unit, ready to tackle the complexities of the digital workspace together.

5

Nurturing Inclusivity in a Remote Environment

"Diversity is being invited to the party; inclusivity is being asked to dance."
— Verna Myers

I n the vast expanse of the digital workplace, where geographical boundaries blur, the fabric of inclusivity becomes crucial in weaving together distributed and global teams. As entrepreneurs venture into the digital age, the creation of an inclusive work environment demands deliberate action and commitment. This chapter delves into the essence of inclusivity within remote teams, underscoring its pivotal role in harnessing the collective strength of diverse talents and perspectives. By fostering an environment that champions equality, respect, and a sense of belonging, leaders can unlock the rich tapestry of creativity and innovation inherent in their teams.

The journey towards inclusivity in a remote setting is fraught with unique challenges—from bridging cultural differences to dismantling communication barriers. Yet, it is within these challenges that the opportunity for transformation lies. Entrepreneurs must navigate these waters with empathy, understanding, and a strategic approach to cultivate a culture where every team member, regardless of their background or location, feels valued and empowered to contribute fully. This chapter outlines practical strategies for embedding inclusivity into the core of remote work environments, ensuring that diversity is not just present but actively celebrated and leveraged for collective success.

Creating a culture of inclusivity in remote teams is not a one-time initiative but a continuous endeavor. It requires leaders to be vigilant against biases, to promote psychological safety, and to ensure that opportunities for growth and recognition are equitably distributed. Through a combination of clear values, proactive communication, and inclusive policies, entrepreneurs can nurture a remote work environment that not only values diversity but thrives on it. This chapter provides a roadmap for leaders to embark on this transformative journey, shaping remote teams that are not only inclusive but also high-performing and resilient.

To establish inclusivity as a cornerstone of remote work culture, entrepreneurs must first lay down values that celebrate diversity and equality. These values should not only be stated but actively practiced, with leaders modeling inclusive behavior and setting expectations for the entire team.

Psychological safety, the bedrock of innovative and open teams, becomes even more critical in a remote setting. Leaders must foster an environment where team members feel safe to voice their ideas and concerns, knowing they will be met with respect and open-mindedness.

Bias and stereotypes, often embedded in workplace practices unconsciously, must be actively identified and addressed. Through initiatives like bias training and diverse hiring panels, leaders can work towards a more equitable and inclusive remote work environment.

Opening Anecdote: Adobe's Flexible Foundations

Adobe's approach to inclusivity in its remote work policies showcases the profound impact of flexibility and understanding in fostering an inclusive environment. By accommodating individual needs and promoting a healthy work-life balance, Adobe creates a space where all employees feel supported and valued. Their commitment to diversity and inclusion education, alongside their encouragement of employee-driven initiatives, exemplifies how inclusivity can be nurtured even in sprawling, globally distributed teams.

> ### Quick Thought:
> *Inclusivity in remote teams is the lens through which the diversity of experiences and perspectives can be focused into a powerful beam of innovation and collaboration.*

Entrepreneurship in Action: Key Ingredients

- **Clear Communication of Inclusive Values:** Articulate and demonstrate inclusivity through every layer of team interaction and decision-making.
- **Active Efforts to Mitigate Bias:** Employ strategies and practices that recognize and reduce unconscious bias,

fostering a culture of fairness and respect.

- **Empowerment Through Equal Opportunities:** Ensure all team members have access to growth, development, and recognition, celebrating diversity as a strength.

Case Study: Salesforce's Trailblazing Path to Inclusivity

Salesforce, a global leader in CRM solutions, has set a gold standard in fostering inclusivity within a remote work environment, proving that physical distances do not hinder the cultivation of a deeply inclusive culture. Under the visionary leadership of Marc Benioff, Salesforce has not only championed the integration of technology to streamline operations but also to bridge cultural gaps, ensuring every employee feels valued, heard, and empowered.

Foundation of Inclusivity: Salesforce's journey towards an inclusive remote culture began with the clear articulation of its core values, with equality and trust at the forefront. Recognizing the diversity of its global workforce as a potent source of innovation and strength, the company embarked on a mission to ensure these values permeate every aspect of its operations.

Employee Resource Groups (ERGs): A cornerstone of Salesforce's inclusivity efforts is its robust network of Employee Resource Groups (ERGs). These groups serve as vibrant communities for underrepresented employees, offering a platform for support, professional development, and advocacy. Each ERG, led by passionate employees, is a testament to Salesforce's commitment to celebrating diversity and building a culture of belonging.

Leadership and Learning: Understanding that leadership plays a pivotal role in nurturing an inclusive environment, Salesforce has invested in comprehensive leadership training programs focused on inclusivity and cultural competence. These initiatives equip leaders with the tools and understanding necessary to manage and inspire a diverse, distributed workforce.

Inclusive Hiring Practices: Salesforce's commitment to inclusivity extends to its hiring practices, where the company employs strategies aimed at reducing unconscious bias and ensuring a diverse pool of candidates. This approach not only enriches the organization's cultural fabric but also drives creativity and innovation by bringing a multitude of perspectives to the table.

Impact and Evolution: The impact of Salesforce's efforts on inclusivity has been profound, both internally and within the tech industry at large. By openly sharing their successes and learnings, Salesforce has encouraged other organizations to follow suit, amplifying the importance of inclusivity across the digital workplace.

Salesforce's inclusivity initiatives, particularly its ERGs and leadership training programs, embody the multifaceted approach required to cultivate an environment where every team member, irrespective of their location or background, can thrive. Their story is a beacon for companies navigating the complexities of remote work, demonstrating that with commitment, empathy, and strategic action, creating an inclusive culture is not only possible but essential for success in the digital age.

This case study illustrates the transformative power of leadership committed to inclusivity, offering actionable insights for organizations striving to foster a more inclusive, diverse, and empowered workforce. Salesforce's journey underscores the enduring impact of building a work culture that values every individual's contribution, setting a benchmark for inclusivity in the digital workspace.

```
Pro Tip:
Encourage and facilitate cross-cultural exchanges
among team members. Such interactions can enhance
understanding, reduce biases, and build a genuinely
inclusive team environment.
```

Exercise: Enhancing Inclusivity in Virtual Teams

Developing Bias Awareness and Cultural Sensitivity:

- **Interactive Bias Recognition Session:** Facilitate an interactive workshop where team members can learn about different types of biases—conscious and unconscious. Utilize case studies and real-life scenarios to illustrate how biases might manifest in remote work settings and discuss strategies for mitigating them.
- **Cultural Sensitivity Training:** Organize a series of training sessions aimed at enhancing cultural sensitivity within your team. Cover key topics such as cross-cultural communication, etiquette, and the importance of cultural celebrations. Encourage team members to share their own experiences and learnings.

Fostering Openness and Psychological Safety:

- **Psychological Safety Building Activities:** Initiate activities that promote psychological safety, such as 'Failure Forums' where team members can share mistakes and learnings in a supportive environment, or 'Ask Me Anything' sessions with leadership to encourage openness and vulnerability.
- **Inclusive Policy Review Session:** Conduct a workshop with your team to review and co-create inclusive policies and practices. Focus on flexible work arrangements, anti-discrimination policies, and mechanisms for reporting and addressing grievances.

Promoting Equality and Recognition:

- **Equal Opportunities Audit:** Lead an audit of your current practices and policies to identify any gaps in providing equal opportunities for growth, development, and recognition. Use findings to develop an action plan addressing these gaps.
- **Diversity Celebration Series:** Launch a monthly series celebrating the diverse backgrounds of your team members. Include virtual events that highlight different cultures, traditions, and stories, fostering a sense of belonging and appreciation among team members.

Challenge for You:
Select a focus area—bias awareness and cultural sensitivity, fostering openness and psychological safety, or promoting equality and recognition. Over the next three months, imple-

ment targeted strategies from this workshop aimed at enhancing inclusivity in your virtual team. Document the process, observe changes in team dynamics, and collect feedback from team members on the effectiveness of these initiatives. Share outcomes and lessons learned with the broader organization to encourage a company-wide commitment to inclusivity.

Concluding Thoughts:

As we conclude this exploration of nurturing inclusivity in a remote environment, it's evident that the journey towards creating an inclusive digital workspace is both complex and rewarding. Leaders are called to act with intentionality, fostering a culture where every team member is empowered to bring their whole selves to work, transcending geographical and cultural boundaries. This chapter has equipped you with strategies and insights to cultivate a workplace where diversity is not only recognized but celebrated as a source of strength and innovation. Moving forward, the challenge lies in consistently applying these principles, ensuring that inclusivity becomes the bedrock of your organizational culture. By embracing inclusivity, you pave the way for a more dynamic, creative, and unified team, ready to thrive in the digital age. Are you prepared to lead this charge, transforming your remote workplace into a beacon of inclusivity and collaboration?

6

Overcoming Communication Barriers in a Distributed Setting

"The art of communication is the language of leadership."
— James Humes

I n the fabric of the digital workspace, where teams are dispersed across continents, effective communication emerges as the linchpin holding the threads of collaboration and leadership together. The unique landscape of distributed teams, marked by diverse time zones, cultures, and communication styles, presents both challenges and opportunities for entrepreneurs. This chapter embarks on a journey to dissect these communication barriers, offering a beacon for leaders striving to cultivate clear, efficient, and inclusive channels of communication within their virtual teams.

The essence of overcoming communication barriers in a distributed setting lies in recognizing the multifaceted nature of these obstacles—from the tangible, such as physical distance and time zone discrepancies, to the more nuanced, like cultural and linguistic diversity. Each layer adds complexity to the task of ensuring messages are not just transmitted but accurately received and understood. Entrepreneurs are called upon to be architects of a communication strategy that bridges these gaps, fostering an environment where every team member feels connected, heard, and valued.

Adopting a strategic approach to communication in distributed teams involves more than just selecting the right tools; it demands an ethos of active listening, empathy, and adaptability. By weaving together technology, cultural sensitivity, and inclusive practices, leaders can overcome the inherent challenges of remote collaboration. This chapter outlines practical steps for entrepreneurs to build robust communication frameworks that enhance clarity, foster trust, and drive team performance, regardless of the physical distances that separate them.

Addressing communication challenges in distributed teams begins with acknowledging the impact of physical distance on the quality of interactions. Entrepreneurs must proactively create opportunities for face-to-face communication via video conferencing and implement regular check-ins to mitigate the effects of separation.

Cultural and language differences, while potential barriers, also offer a rich tapestry of perspectives that, when navigated with care, can enhance team creativity and problem-solving. Establishing clear communication channels, guidelines, and fostering an environment of active listening and clarification are foundational steps in building a bridge over these divides.

Opening Anecdote: Shopify's Communication Compass

Shopify, a leader in the e-commerce space, exemplifies the power of strategic communication within distributed teams. Through regular check-ins, asynchronous communication practices, and a commitment to cross-cultural training, Shopify ensures that every team member, no matter their location, feels in sync with the company's heartbeat. Their approach underscores the importance of tailored communication strategies in building a cohesive and productive remote workforce.

> **Quick Thought:**
> *Effective communication in distributed teams is akin to conducting an orchestra—each instrument, though playing from a different sheet of music, contributes to a harmonious symphony under the guidance of a skilled conductor.*

Entrepreneurship in Action: Key Ingredients

- **Clear Communication Protocols:** Establish and communicate guidelines for how, when, and where team communications should take place, respecting time zones and work-life balance.
- **Active Listening and Empathy:** Promote practices that ensure every team member feels heard and understood, fostering a culture of empathy and mutual respect.
- **Leverage of Technology:** Select and utilize communica-

tion tools that fit the unique needs of your team, ensuring accessibility and ease of use for all members.

Case Study: Zoom's Convergence of Technology and Human Connection

In an era where remote work has transcended from a mere possibility to a global norm, Zoom stands out not just as a tool, but as a harbinger of effective communication across distributed teams. Under the leadership of Eric Yuan, Zoom's journey from a startup to a household name in video conferencing is a testament to overcoming communication barriers in a digital workspace.

Strategic Vision: Eric Yuan's vision was clear from the outset: to create a video conferencing platform that not only bridged geographical distances but also fostered a sense of connection and inclusivity. Recognizing the multifaceted challenges of remote communication—from time zone discrepancies to cultural and linguistic diversity—Zoom was designed to be more than a tool; it aimed to be a solution that enhances human connection in the digital age.

Features Fostering Inclusivity: Zoom's array of features, including virtual whiteboards, breakout rooms, and real-time multilingual captioning, exemplify its commitment to inclusivity. These features are not just technological advancements but strategic tools to overcome common barriers in remote communication, enabling diverse teams to collaborate effectively and empathetically.

Adapting to Global Needs: Understanding the global nature of modern teams, Zoom has continuously evolved, introducing features that cater to a wide array of communication styles and needs. The platform's ability to support large-scale meetings with participants from various cultural backgrounds while maintaining high-quality audio and video has made it an indispensable tool for companies navigating the complexities of distributed teamwork.

Cultural Sensitivity and Flexibility: Under Yuan's leadership, Zoom has emphasized the importance of cultural sensitivity, integrating features that respect and celebrate global diversity. This approach has not only enhanced Zoom's utility as a communication tool but has also positioned it as a leader in promoting understanding and respect among distributed teams.

Empowering Leaders and Teams: Zoom's success story extends beyond its technical capabilities; it is also about empowering leaders and teams to cultivate a culture of clear, efficient, and inclusive communication. By providing a platform that addresses the core challenges of remote collaboration, Zoom enables leaders to focus on what truly matters—building trust, fostering collaboration, and driving team performance.

Zoom's blueprint for success demonstrates how technology, when thoughtfully designed and implemented, can transcend the barriers of distance, language, and culture, promoting a more inclusive and collaborative remote work environment. Its journey offers valuable lessons for entrepreneurs striving to enhance communication within their distributed teams, highlighting the importance of empathy, adaptability, and a deep commitment to connecting people in the digital age.

This case study illuminates the path for leaders seeking to navigate the communication challenges of distributed settings, emphasizing that the key to overcoming these obstacles lies in leveraging technology with a human-centric approach. Zoom's story is a powerful reminder that at the heart of effective communication lies the unwavering pursuit of human connection and understanding, bridging the digital divide to create a unified, collaborative, and inclusive work culture.

```
Pro Tip:
Encourage the use of visual communication tools,
such as infographics and shared digital workspaces,
to complement verbal and written communication,
enhancing clarity and engagement.
```

Exercise: Mastering Communication in Distributed Teams

Virtual Communication Mastery:

- **Interactive Virtual Meeting Facilitation:** Host a comprehensive training session on effective virtual meeting facilitation. Cover essential aspects like setting clear agendas, utilizing engagement tools (polls, breakout rooms), and ensuring every voice is heard. Include scenarios that require adaptability and showcase best practices for maintaining engagement in a virtual setting.
- **Empathy and Active Listening Seminar:** Design a seminar focusing on empathy and active listening in a remote environment. Utilize role-playing exercises to practice these skills, emphasizing understanding non-

verbal cues in a virtual context and responding to team members' needs and feedback effectively.

Cultural and Linguistic Inclusivity:

- **Cross-Cultural Communication Workshop:** Implement a workshop that explores the nuances of cross-cultural communication. Include sessions on understanding cultural norms, avoiding common misunderstandings, and using inclusive language. Incorporate interactive activities that encourage team members to share their cultural backgrounds and communication preferences.
- **Language Flexibility Initiatives:** Organize language appreciation days where team members can share common phrases in their languages, promoting linguistic diversity. Provide access to language learning resources or apps to encourage team members to learn basics in each other's languages, fostering a deeper sense of connection and effort.

Leveraging Technology for Better Communication:

- **Tech-Savvy Communication Clinic:** Conduct a clinic to review and train team members on the array of communication tools available. Focus on maximizing the features of these tools to enhance team collaboration, such as shared calendars for scheduling across time zones, project management software for transparent task tracking, and instant messaging apps for real-time communication.
- **Visual Communication Tactics Session:** Host a session on the power of visual communication tools. Train

team members on creating and interpreting infographics, engaging with shared digital workspaces, and utilizing visual aids in presentations to overcome language and cultural barriers.

Challenge for You:

Select an area of focus—Virtual Communication Mastery, Cultural and Linguistic Inclusivity, or Leveraging Technology for Better Communication. Over the following month, apply targeted strategies from this workshop to address a communication challenge within your team. Engage in a reflective practice to document the strategy's effectiveness, the team's response, and observed changes in communication dynamics. Share your findings and adjustments made based on feedback, fostering a culture of continuous improvement in communication practices.

Concluding Thoughts:

As we draw this chapter to a close, it's clear that mastering the art of communication in a distributed setting is foundational to the success of remote teams. This exploration has equipped you with the strategies and insights necessary to bridge the gaps that distance can create, fostering a culture of open, empathetic, and effective communication. By embracing the diversity of your team and leveraging technology wisely, you have the opportunity to transform potential obstacles into strengths, enhancing collaboration and unity across borders. The journey ahead will require continuous learning, adaptability, and a commitment to nurturing the connections that make your team unique. Are you ready to lead with a communication style that not only transcends physical distances but also deeply connects with every member of your team, paving the way for unprecedented collaboration and success in the digital age?

7

Leveraging Technology for Effective Virtual Communication

"Innovation is facilitated by having the right people in the right roles with the right skills and values."
— Charles Koch

As digital landscapes continue to evolve, the pivotal role of technology in bridging the communication divide within distributed teams becomes increasingly apparent. This chapter navigates through the myriad of technological solutions available to entrepreneurs, aiming to transform the virtual communication experience from a mere necessity into a dynamic, engaging, and productive environment. It underscores the significance of selecting and utilizing the right mix of tools that not only overcome physical distances but also enrich interactions, fostering a cohesive and vibrant team culture.

The advent of video conferencing platforms, instant messaging apps, collaborative editing tools, and project management software has revolutionized the way remote teams communicate and collaborate. These technologies offer a lifeline for maintaining the human connection essential for team spirit and collaboration in a virtual workspace. However, the abundance of options necessitates a strategic approach to choosing tools that align with the team's specific needs, enhancing efficiency without overwhelming users with complexity. This chapter delves into the criteria for selecting these technologies and optimizing their use to maximize the benefits of virtual communication.

Beyond the selection of tools, the chapter also explores the nuances of facilitating clear, inclusive, and effective communication across diverse and geographically dispersed teams. It highlights the importance of adapting communication strategies to fit the cultural, linguistic, and individual preferences of team members, ensuring that technology serves as a bridge rather than a barrier. Through practical tips and real-world examples, entrepreneurs are guided on how to create a virtual communication ecosystem that supports transparency, collaboration, and inclusivity.

Choosing the right communication tools involves a balance between functionality and user-friendliness. Video conferencing platforms like Zoom and Microsoft Teams offer a visual connection, while instant messaging apps such as Slack and Discord support real-time, informal interactions. Entrepreneurs are encouraged to consider their team's specific communication needs and preferences when selecting these tools.

Collaborative document sharing and project management tools, including Google Drive and Trello, eliminate the chaos of version control and task delegation, enabling teams to work together seamlessly despite physical separation. Virtual whiteboarding platforms and diagramming tools further support visual collaboration, catering to diverse thinking and planning styles within the team.

Opening Anecdote: Asana's Collaborative Pulse

Asana's implementation of a comprehensive suite of communication and collaboration tools exemplifies the transformative power of technology in virtual workspaces. By facilitating task management, file sharing, and team communication within a single platform, Asana not only streamlines workflows but also fosters a sense of unity and purpose among distributed team members. Their approach illuminates the path for entrepreneurs seeking to harness technology to enhance team dynamics and drive project success.

> **Quick Thought:**
> *Effective virtual communication transcends technological proficiency; it requires a commitment to creating an inclusive and engaging environment that values every team member's input and perspective.*

Entrepreneurship in Action: Key Ingredients

- **Strategic Selection of Tools:** Evaluate and choose communication technologies that align with your team's size, workflow, and objectives.
- **Encouragement of Active Participation:** Foster a culture where team members feel comfortable and encouraged to share their ideas and feedback using these tools.

- **Continuous Adaptation and Training:** Provide ongoing support and training to ensure all team members can effectively use the selected communication tools.

Case Study: Slack's Seamless Symphony

Slack's journey from a simple messaging tool to a cornerstone of virtual communication in distributed teams exemplifies the transformative power of technology in overcoming communication barriers. Founded by Stewart Butterfield, Slack began as an internal communication tool for his team at Tiny Speck during the development of an online game. Recognizing its potential to solve broader communication challenges faced by remote teams, Butterfield pivoted to develop Slack into a platform that today serves millions worldwide.

Foundational Vision: Butterfield's vision for Slack was clear: to create a platform that not only facilitated instant messaging but also organized conversations in a way that made work life simpler, more pleasant, and more productive. Slack's innovative channel-based messaging system was designed to bring team communication and collaboration into one place, significantly reducing the need for emails and enabling teams to work more transparently.

Empowering Distributed Teams: Slack's impact on remote work communication is profound. By providing teams with the ability to create channels for different projects, topics, or departments, Slack ensures that relevant conversations and files are neatly organized and easily accessible. This structure empowers distributed teams to stay aligned, informed, and responsive, regardless of physical location.

Enhancing Connectivity and Inclusivity: Under Butterfield's leadership, Slack has continuously evolved to enhance its inclusivity and connectivity features, such as integrating video calling capabilities, file sharing, and third-party app integrations. These features allow teams to customize their workflow and communication style, fostering a sense of community and collaboration. Slack's emphasis on creating a user-friendly interface and its commitment to maintaining a secure and reliable platform further cement its role as an indispensable tool for remote teams.

Driving Innovation and Adaptability: Slack's ability to adapt and innovate in response to the needs of its diverse user base has been central to its success. The platform's flexibility and scalability make it suitable for small teams and large enterprises alike, proving that effective communication in a distributed setting is not just about sharing information but about creating a shared space for collaboration, creativity, and cohesion.

Slack's blueprint for success lies in its understanding that the essence of effective virtual communication transcends technological proficiency; it requires building an inclusive and engaging environment that values every team member's input and perspective. As remote work continues to evolve, Slack's commitment to improving and innovating its platform ensures it remains at the forefront of facilitating not just communication, but the very culture of distributed teamwork.

```
Pro Tip:
Regularly review and assess the effectiveness of
```

```
your communication tools. Be open to feedback from
team members and ready to adapt your technology
stack to meet evolving needs and challenges.
```

Exercise: Technology-Driven Communication Mastery

Optimizing Your Tech Stack for Communication:

- **Comprehensive Technology Review Session:** Conduct a detailed assessment of your existing communication tools to identify overlaps, gaps, and underutilized features. This session should culminate in a strategic plan for streamlining your tech stack to better meet your team's communication needs.
- **Tool Tutorial Marathon:** Organize a series of interactive tutorials covering the most effective use of selected communication tools. Focus on hidden features and integrations that can enhance team collaboration and productivity. Encourage team members to share their tips and tricks for using these tools in their daily workflows.

Fostering Inclusive and Clear Communication:

- **Inclusive Communication Workshop:** Develop a workshop aimed at fostering inclusive communication practices within your team. Include training on language sensitivity, cultural awareness, and accommodating different communication styles to ensure every team member can engage fully and effectively.

- **Clear Communication Challenges:** Initiate a month-long challenge focusing on clear and concise communication. Encourage team members to practice summarizing their messages and ensuring key points are well articulated and understood, using both asynchronous and synchronous tools.

Adapting and Training for Continuous Improvement:

- **Feedback and Adaptation Session:** Create a structured feedback session for team members to voice their experiences with current communication tools and processes. Use this feedback to adapt and evolve your communication strategies, ensuring they remain aligned with team needs and preferences.
- **Ongoing Learning Commitment:** Pledge to continuous learning and adaptation in the realm of virtual communication. Set up quarterly review meetings to discuss new tools, emerging best practices, and ongoing training needs to keep your team at the forefront of effective digital collaboration.

Challenge for You:

Select an area for improvement—Optimizing Your Tech Stack, Fostering Inclusive and Clear Communication, or Adapting and Training for Continuous Improvement. Over the next three months, implement a focused initiative based on insights from this workshop. Track the initiative's impact on enhancing virtual communication and team dynamics. Conclude with a team debrief to gather feedback and identify next steps for further improvement.

Concluding Thoughts:

As we conclude this exploration of leveraging technology for effective virtual communication, it's evident that the journey is as much about the people as it is about the tools. The thoughtful selection, implementation, and continuous refinement of communication technologies serve as the bedrock upon which dynamic, inclusive, and productive remote teams are built. This chapter has armed you with the insights and strategies necessary to foster an environment where every team member can thrive, bridging the gap between technology and human connection. The path forward requires a commitment to embracing change, fostering open dialogue, and continuously seeking ways to enhance the virtual communication landscape. Are you ready to step into this future, leading with innovation and a deep understanding of the transformative power of technology in connecting us all?

8

Fostering Engagement and Team Cohesion Across Time Zones

"Leadership is the challenge to be something more than average."
— Jim Rohn

N avigating the complexities of a distributed work-force requires more than just managing tasks and workflows; it demands a deep understanding of how time zones impact team dynamics and communication. This chapter dives into the heart of fostering engagement and team cohesion across the vast expanse of global time differences. By dissecting the nuances of time zone management, entrepreneurs are equipped with the strategies to cultivate a work environment where every team member, regardless of their geographic location, feels connected, valued, and an integral part of the team's collective success.

The challenge of time zone diversity is twofold: it poses logistical hurdles in scheduling and communication, yet offers a unique opportunity to harness the benefits of a nearly 24-

hour operation cycle. Entrepreneurs and leaders are tasked with the delicate balance of maximizing the advantages while mitigating the downsides of distributed teams. This chapter outlines practical approaches to embrace time zone awareness, establish effective communication protocols, and ensure that all team members are engaged and contributing to their fullest potential despite the physical and temporal distances that separate them.

Creating a cohesive team environment across time zones goes beyond mere scheduling flexibility; it involves fostering a culture of inclusivity, understanding, and mutual respect. Through strategic meeting management, clear and transparent communication, and the promotion of flexibility and work-life balance, leaders can build a foundation of trust and collaboration that transcends geographical boundaries. This chapter provides a blueprint for entrepreneurs to navigate the challenges of time zone differences, paving the way for a unified, productive, and engaged distributed team.

To effectively manage time zone variations, entrepreneurs must become adept at visualizing and planning around the global clock. Tools like World Time Buddy offer invaluable assistance in this regard, enabling leaders to schedule meetings and deadlines with sensitivity to everyone's local working hours.

Clear communication protocols are essential in a distributed team, particularly when navigating time zone differences. Establishing guidelines for asynchronous communication ensures that team members can contribute meaningfully without being constrained by the immediate availability of their colleagues.

Opening Anecdote: The Siemens Connective Strategy

Siemens, a global powerhouse in technology and engineering, showcases the epitome of fostering engagement and team cohesion across myriad time zones. With operations spanning across continents, Siemens has crafted a connective strategy that relies on a mix of synchronous and asynchronous communication tools, underpinned by a strong culture of flexibility and inclusivity. This approach ensures that every team member, irrespective of their geographic location, feels an integral part of the company's pulsating rhythm. Siemens' commitment to creating a seamless global work environment stands as a testament to the achievable harmony in a well-orchestrated distributed team.

> **Quick Thought:**
> *The strength of a distributed team lies in its ability to operate across the continuum of time zones, transforming geographic diversity into a competitive advantage rather than a challenge.*

Entrepreneurship in Action: Key Ingredients

- **Embracing Time Zone Diversity:** View time zone differences as an opportunity to extend the team's productive hours, rather than a hurdle.
- **Communication Clarity and Consistency:** Implement clear protocols for communication that cater to the needs of team members in various time zones.

- **Fostering a Culture of Flexibility:** Encourage flexible working arrangements that allow team members to work at times when they are most productive.

Case Study: DocuSign's Harmonized Global Workforce

DocuSign, a pioneer in electronic agreement services, has effectively navigated the complexities of managing a distributed workforce spanning numerous time zones. Under the leadership of CEO Dan Springer, DocuSign has cultivated a culture that not only acknowledges the challenges of global team coordination but also leverages these differences to its strategic advantage.

Strategic Initiatives for Inclusivity: At the core of DocuSign's strategy is a commitment to inclusivity and flexibility. Recognizing the potential strain of time zone disparities on team cohesion and individual work-life balance, Springer's leadership team implemented a rotating schedule for all-hands meetings and critical discussions. This approach ensures that no single region consistently bears the inconvenience of off-hours meetings, fostering a sense of fairness and respect across the workforce.

Leveraging Asynchronous Communication: DocuSign's embrace of asynchronous communication channels stands as a testament to its innovative approach to global team management. By encouraging the use of comprehensive documentation, recorded meetings, and clear, detailed project updates, the company ensures that team members remain informed and engaged, irrespective of their geographic location. This method not only enhances productivity but also respects individual work patterns and personal commitments, contributing to higher job satisfaction and team morale.

Empowering Through Technology: Technology plays a pivotal role in DocuSign's strategy to overcome time zone barriers. The company employs a suite of collaboration tools that facilitate seamless communication and project management. From video conferencing software that supports recorded sessions to project management platforms enabling real-time updates, DocuSign equips its teams with the resources necessary to collaborate effectively, regardless of physical distance.

Cultural Sensitivity and Flexibility: Under Springer's direction, DocuSign places a high value on cultural sensitivity and flexibility, acknowledging the diverse cultural backgrounds of its global workforce. The company's policies and initiatives are designed to celebrate this diversity, from recognizing international holidays to providing language support and cross-cultural training. This not only enhances team cohesion but also enriches the company's collective creativity and problem-solving capabilities.

DocuSign's approach to fostering engagement and team cohesion across time zones offers valuable lessons for any leader navigating the digital age's challenges. By prioritizing inclusivity, leveraging asynchronous communication, utilizing technology, and celebrating cultural diversity, DocuSign has demonstrated that distributed teams can not only function efficiently but can thrive. Springer's leadership has shown that with the right strategies, the challenges posed by global time differences can be transformed into opportunities for innovation, engagement, and sustained organizational growth.

```
Pro Tip:
Rotate meeting times to share the inconvenience of
non-ideal hours equitably among team members,
demonstrating fairness and respect for everyone's
work-life balance.
```

Exercise: Mastering Time Zone Harmony

Strategies for Time Zone Management:

- **Time Zone Visualization Activity:** Conduct a session where team members plot their locations on a world map, identifying overlapping work hours. This visual aid serves to enhance empathy and understanding among team members, facilitating the scheduling of meetings and collaborative work periods.
- **Scheduling Equity Exercise:** Develop a rotating schedule for team meetings and check-ins that distributes meeting times fairly across different time zones. This exercise encourages leaders to be mindful of the diverse needs and challenges faced by team members in various regions, promoting inclusivity and respect.

Enhancing Asynchronous Workflows:

- **Asynchronous Work Best Practices Workshop:** Share strategies and tools for effective asynchronous collaboration, emphasizing how to maintain productivity and engagement without real-time interaction. Highlight case studies or examples of successful asynchronous projects within your team or other organizations.

- **Collaboration Platform Deep Dive:** Choose a collaboration tool used by your team (e.g., Slack, Trello, Asana) and explore its features in depth, focusing on those that support asynchronous work. Encourage team members to share tips and tricks they've discovered that enhance asynchronous collaboration.

Building Engagement and Cohesion Across Distances:

- **Virtual Team Building Event:** Organize an interactive virtual event that does not rely on all members being present simultaneously. Consider activities that can be accessed and enjoyed over a span of 24-48 hours, allowing participation from all time zones.
- **Feedback and Flexibility Forum:** Create a space for team members to share their experiences and suggestions regarding time zone management, work flexibility, and asynchronous work. Use this feedback to adapt and refine your team's approach to working across time zones.

Challenge for You:

Select one focus area—Strategies for Time Zone Management, Enhancing Asynchronous Workflows, or Building Engagement and Cohesion Across Distances. Over the next two months, implement a targeted initiative that aims to address challenges or capitalize on opportunities within that area. Monitor the initiative's impact on team dynamics, productivity, and morale. Conclude with a reflective session to discuss lessons learned and identify future actions to further improve time zone inclusivity and team cohesion.

Concluding Thoughts:

The journey through fostering engagement and team cohesion across time zones concludes with a forward-looking perspective, emphasizing the transformative power of embracing global diversity. As leaders, the challenge to bridge time zones not only tests our logistical acumen but also our ability to innovate in fostering connection and unity within our teams. This chapter has armed you with the strategies and insights needed to turn geographical dispersion into a strategic advantage, promoting a culture where every team member, irrespective of their location, feels integral to the collective mission. The path forward is paved with opportunities for growth, innovation, and deeper collaboration, inviting leaders to champion a work environment that thrives on inclusivity, flexibility, and shared success. Are you ready to embrace this journey, leading your global team towards a future where distance is no barrier to achieving remarkable things together?

9

Navigating Cross-Cultural Communication Challenges

"Culture is the widening of the mind and of the spirit."
— Jawaharlal Nehru

In the tapestry of today's global work environment, the threads of diverse cultures weave a complex pattern, presenting both challenges and opportunities for communication within distributed teams. This chapter delves into the heart of cross-cultural communication, unpacking the layers of cultural intelligence required to navigate the intricate dynamics of global teams. By embracing the rich tapestry of cultural diversity, entrepreneurs can unlock unparalleled levels of team inclusivity, minimize misunderstandings, and propel team productivity to new heights.

Cultural intelligence emerges not just as a skill but as a vital component of effective leadership in the digital age. It extends beyond the acknowledgment of cultural differences to the active adaptation and integration of diverse cultural perspectives into the communication fabric of distributed teams. This chapter outlines strategies for cultivating cultural sensitivity, overcoming language barriers, and harnessing the power of nonverbal communication cues, equipping entrepreneurs with the tools to foster a genuinely inclusive and collaborative work environment.

The journey through cross-cultural communication is paved with challenges, from direct versus indirect communication styles to the nuances of conflict resolution in a multicultural context. However, it is within these challenges that the opportunity for growth lies. Through active listening, empathy, and a commitment to understanding, entrepreneurs can bridge the cultural divides, transforming potential obstacles into sources of strength and innovation. This chapter provides a roadmap for navigating the complexities of cross-cultural communication, enabling leaders to build teams that are not just connected by technology but united by mutual respect and shared purpose.

To navigate the maze of cultural diversity effectively, entrepreneurs must first lay the groundwork for understanding and appreciating cultural nuances. Tools like the Cultural Intelligence Assessment offer valuable insights into personal and team cultural intelligence levels, providing a starting point for development.

Cultural sensitivity, a cornerstone of effective cross-cultural communication, requires more than an open mindset; it demands active engagement and adaptability. Leaders must champion respect for diverse perspectives and tailor their communication styles to bridge cultural gaps, fostering an environment of trust and mutual respect.

Opening Anecdote: Booking.com's Cultural Compass

Booking.com, with its footprint in countries around the globe, stands as a paragon of cross-cultural communication excellence. Their comprehensive cultural training program for employees underscores a deep commitment to understanding and embracing cultural differences, enhancing interactions with both customers and team members worldwide. This initiative not only facilitates smoother communication but also cultivates an atmosphere where diversity is celebrated, driving the company towards global success.

> **Quick Thought:**
> *Mastering cross-cultural communication in distributed teams transforms perceived barriers into a mosaic of opportunities for growth, innovation, and enhanced team cohesion.*

Entrepreneurship in Action: Key Ingredients

- **Cultivating Cultural Sensitivity:** Embrace and adapt to diverse cultural expressions and communication styles to foster mutual understanding.
- **Enhancing Language Clarity and Support:** Provide language training and utilize translation tools to ensure clear and inclusive communication.
- **Encouraging Empathy and Active Listening:** Promote practices that foster empathy and encourage team members to engage deeply with diverse perspectives.

Case Study: Patagonia's Global Communication Mastery

Patagonia, an outdoor apparel company celebrated for its environmental activism, has also distinguished itself in mastering cross-cultural communication within its globally distributed teams. Under the leadership of CEO Rose Marcario, Patagonia has woven cultural sensitivity and empathy into the fabric of its corporate identity, fostering an environment where diverse perspectives are not just heard but are integral to the company's mission.

Empathy-Driven Leadership: At the heart of Patagonia's approach is an empathy-driven leadership model that recognizes the value of understanding and respecting the cultural backgrounds of all team members. This ethos is reflected in the company's internal training programs, which are designed to cultivate a deep appreciation for cultural diversity among employees. These programs encourage team members to share their cultural insights, enhancing mutual respect and understanding across the organization.

Cultural Exchange Initiatives: Patagonia has implemented a series of cultural exchange initiatives that promote open dialogue and cultural sharing. These initiatives include regular cultural awareness workshops, language learning opportunities, and celebration of global festivals. By integrating these practices into the everyday work environment, Patagonia ensures that cross-cultural communication is not just about overcoming barriers but about enriching the company culture with a wide array of perspectives and experiences.

Adapting Communication Styles: Understanding that

effective communication is key to navigating cultural differences, Patagonia actively adapts its communication styles to meet the needs of its global team. This adaptability extends to recognizing and accommodating various communication preferences, whether they be direct or indirect, and adjusting meeting structures to be inclusive of all participants, regardless of their cultural norms.

Language Support and Inclusion: Recognizing language as a potential barrier to inclusion, Patagonia provides language support services to its employees, including access to translation tools and language training resources. This commitment ensures that all team members can fully engage and contribute, regardless of their native language.

Patagonia's success in fostering effective cross-cultural communication within its distributed teams serves as a blueprint for other global companies. By prioritizing empathy, cultural exchange, and adaptability in communication styles, Patagonia has not only overcome the challenges associated with global team management but has also leveraged its cultural diversity as a source of strength and innovation. Marcario's leadership underscores the importance of building a corporate culture that embraces diversity at every level, demonstrating that true communication mastery in the digital age is rooted in empathy and a genuine appreciation for the richness of global perspectives.

```
Pro Tip:
Implement regular cultural exchange sessions within
```

your team to share and celebrate the diverse
backgrounds of team members, enhancing cultural
understanding and team unity.

Exercise: Enhancing Cross-Cultural Communication

Building Cultural Intelligence:

- **Cultural Quotient Reflection:** Engage in a self-assessment to understand your current level of cultural intelligence. Reflect on scenarios where cultural differences affected communication within your team, and identify areas for growth.
- **Global Perspectives Journal:** Maintain a journal over a month, noting daily learnings about different cultures represented in your team or business network. Focus on insights gained from interactions, readings, or media that contribute to a deeper understanding of these cultures.

Developing Communication Skills Across Cultures:

- **Language Flexibility Exercises:** Participate in language exchange sessions within your team, focusing on learning key phrases or cultural nuances in languages other than your own. This exercise aims to build empathy and reduce language barriers.
- **Non-Verbal Communication Workshop:** Explore the significance of non-verbal cues in different cultures through role-play and case studies. Learn how to interpret

and use non-verbal communication effectively in a multicultural team setting.

Fostering Inclusivity and Empathy:

- **Cultural Insight Presentations:** Organize a series of short presentations where team members share insights about their cultural backgrounds, communication styles, and professional etiquette. This initiative promotes mutual respect and understanding.
- **Empathy Circle:** Conduct virtual meetings where team members discuss personal experiences with cultural misunderstandings or biases, focusing on listening and empathy. Use these sessions to develop strategies for more inclusive communication practices.

Challenge for You:

Select one area—Building Cultural Intelligence, Developing Communication Skills Across Cultures, or Fostering Inclusivity and Empathy. Over the next three months, focus on implementing specific activities from that area within your team. Monitor the impact of these initiatives on enhancing cross-cultural communication and team cohesion. Gather feedback from your team to identify successful strategies and areas needing further attention.

Concluding Thoughts:

As we wrap up our exploration of navigating cross-cultural communication challenges, it's clear that the journey towards fostering an environment of inclusivity and understanding within distributed teams is both complex and rewarding.

By prioritizing cultural intelligence, language clarity, and empathy, leaders can bridge the gaps between diverse team members, creating a workspace where innovation and collaboration flourish. This chapter has laid the groundwork for leaders to appreciate and leverage the rich tapestry of cultures within their teams, transforming potential challenges into opportunities for growth and unity. Embracing the strategies and insights provided here paves the way for a future where teams are not just connected by technology but are bound by a shared sense of purpose and mutual respect. Are you ready to embrace this journey, leveraging the power of diversity to lead your team towards new horizons of success and collaboration?

10

Goal Setting and Performance Management in a Distributed Environment

"Goals are the fuel in the furnace of achievement."
— Brian Tracy

I
n the realm of distributed teams, the clarity of goals and the precision of performance management form the backbone of success. This chapter navigates the nuanced landscape of setting clear, attainable objectives and managing team performance across the digital divide. By crafting a robust framework for goal setting and embracing the power of technology, entrepreneurs can ensure that their teams are not just aligned with the organizational vision but are also driven towards achieving collective excellence, despite the geographical spread.

The challenge of managing performance in a distributed setting goes beyond traditional metrics and evaluations; it requires a deep understanding of each team member's context, the ability to communicate expectations transparently, and the foresight to leverage technology for continuous feedback and progress tracking. This chapter outlines strategic approaches for setting SMART goals that resonate with both the team's and the organization's aspirations, ensuring that everyone is rowing in the same direction. Additionally, it delves into the art of performance management in a virtual landscape, highlighting the importance of key performance indicators (KPIs), regular assessments, and the fostering of a culture of accountability and recognition.

In a distributed environment, the dynamics of goal setting and performance management also encompass the nurturing of autonomy, the promotion of self-management, and the provision of ample opportunities for professional growth and development. Entrepreneurs are tasked with the delicate balance of providing direction and support while empowering their teams to take ownership of their roles and contributions. Through a combination of clear communication, strategic use of performance tracking tools, and a commitment to continuous learning, leaders can cultivate a high-performance culture that thrives on collaboration, innovation, and mutual respect across all time zones.

To navigate the complexities of performance management in a distributed team, entrepreneurs must identify and implement relevant Key Performance Indicators (KPIs) that offer insights into both individual and collective progress. Establishing a regular cadence for performance reviews, incorporating self-assessments, peer evaluations, and managerial feedback, provides a comprehensive view of performance and areas for improvement.

The adoption of performance tracking tools and feedback

platforms is crucial in automating data collection and facilitating real-time insights into team dynamics. Platforms like Asana for project management and Slack for continuous feedback enable leaders to monitor progress and recognize achievements, fostering a motivated and engaged team.

Opening Anecdote: Google's OKR Journey

Google's adoption of the OKR (Objectives and Key Results) framework stands as a testament to the transformative power of goal setting in driving organizational performance. By setting ambitious objectives and measurable key results, Google has fostered a culture of transparency, accountability, and continuous improvement, empowering teams across the globe to align their efforts with the company's overarching goals. This approach not only enhances team cohesion but also propels the organization towards its strategic milestones.

> **Quick Thought:**
> *In the digital age, the effectiveness of goal setting and performance management is amplified by the strategic integration of technology, fostering an environment where distributed teams can excel and innovate.*

Entrepreneurship in Action: Key Ingredients

- **Strategic Goal Alignment:** Ensure that individual and team goals are intricately aligned with the organizational vision, promoting a unified direction.
- **Transparent Communication of Expectations:** Clearly

articulate performance expectations, leveraging digital tools to maintain clarity and consistency across distributed teams.

- **Empowerment through Autonomy:** Foster an environment where team members are encouraged to manage their responsibilities, supported by regular coaching and development opportunities.

Case Study: HubSpot's Performance-Driven Culture

HubSpot, a leading inbound marketing, sales, and service software provider, has pioneered a performance-driven culture that seamlessly blends goal setting with employee development, particularly in its distributed environment. Under the leadership of Brian Halligan and Dharmesh Shah, HubSpot has embraced a transparent and flexible approach to performance management that emphasizes individual growth as much as organizational achievements.

Embracing SMART Goals: HubSpot's adoption of SMART (Specific, Measurable, Achievable, Relevant, Time-Bound) goals is central to its strategy, ensuring every team member, from Boston to Berlin, understands what success looks like. This clarity is achieved through regular, open discussions about goals at every level of the organization, supported by a technology infrastructure that keeps these objectives in the forefront of daily operations.

Technology-Enhanced Performance Tracking: Leveraging technology for performance management, HubSpot utilizes platforms like Lattice for setting objectives and key results (OKRs), facilitating continuous feedback, and tracking progress. This system allows for a dynamic approach to performance reviews, moving beyond annual assessments to more frequent check-ins that reflect the pace of change within the digital marketing landscape.

Cultivating a Culture of Continuous Learning: A cornerstone of HubSpot's approach is its commitment to continuous learning and development. The HubSpot Academy offers employees access to a wealth of online courses and certifications, encouraging them to expand their skills in alignment with their personal and professional goals. This emphasis on growth contributes to a highly motivated workforce that is equipped to meet the evolving demands of their roles.

Fostering Autonomy and Flexibility: Recognizing the diverse needs and preferences of its global team, HubSpot promotes autonomy and flexibility, allowing employees to tailor their work schedules and environments to suit their productivity peaks and life commitments. This trust-based approach is key to maintaining high levels of engagement and performance across time zones.

HubSpot's success in managing a globally distributed team highlights the effectiveness of integrating clear goal setting with flexible performance management practices. By prioritizing transparency, leveraging technology, and fostering a culture of continuous learning, HubSpot not only achieves its organizational objectives but also supports the individual aspirations of its team members. This case study serves as an inspiration for leaders looking to navigate the complexities of goal setting and performance management in a distributed environment, offering a blueprint for creating a cohesive, high-performing team that is aligned with both individual growth and company success.

Pro Tip:
Rotate the focus of performance reviews from solely
outcomes to include behavioral and developmental
aspects, ensuring a holistic approach to growth and
improvement within distributed teams.

Exercise: Distributed Performance Mastery

Strategic Goal Setting:

- **Interactive Goal-Setting Seminar:** Facilitate an interactive virtual seminar where team members collaborate to define SMART (Specific, Measurable, Achievable, Relevant, Time-Bound) goals that align with both personal career aspirations and the organization's vision. This seminar encourages participation through breakout sessions, where smaller groups work on goal-setting exercises and share their outcomes with the larger group.
- **OKR Planning Session:** Organize a workshop focused on developing Objectives and Key Results (OKRs) for various teams within your organization. Utilize collaborative tools to draft OKRs, ensuring they are challenging yet attainable, and clearly linked to the company's strategic priorities. Encourage teams to present their OKRs, fostering a sense of ownership and transparency.

Performance Management Techniques:

- **KPI Dashboard Development:** Guide team leaders through a hands-on session to create customized Key Performance Indicator (KPI) dashboards using performance tracking software. This session should cover the selection of relevant KPIs, dashboard customization, and interpretation of data to make informed management decisions.
- **Feedback Loop Workshop:** Conduct a workshop on establishing effective feedback loops within remote teams. Cover best practices for giving and receiving feedback, the use of technology in facilitating real-time feedback, and strategies to ensure feedback leads to actionable insights and professional development.

Enhancing Team Engagement:

- **Virtual Recognition Ceremony:** Plan and execute a virtual recognition ceremony to celebrate team achievements and individual contributions. This event should highlight the accomplishments related to the set goals and OKRs, and include peer recognition moments to enhance team morale and cohesion.
- **Professional Development Planning:** Host a planning session for team members to identify and commit to professional development activities aligned with their goals. This could involve mentorship pairings, enrollment in online courses, or attendance at virtual conferences. Provide resources or budgets where possible to support these initiatives.

Challenge for You:

Choose two areas—Strategic Goal Setting, Performance Management Techniques, or Enhancing Team Engagement. Implement specific activities from these areas within your team over the next six months. Document the process, including the challenges faced and the impact on team alignment, performance, and engagement. Utilize feedback from your team to refine these practices, creating a robust framework for goal setting and performance management in your distributed environment.

Concluding Thoughts:

In wrapping up our discussion on goal setting and performance management within distributed teams, we are reminded of the transformative power of clearly defined objectives and the strategic application of technology in uniting geographically dispersed talent. This chapter has laid the groundwork for leaders to cultivate an environment where every team member, regardless of location, is deeply engaged and aligned with the organization's aspirations. The path forward requires a steadfast commitment to fostering open communication, embracing cultural diversity, and continuously seeking ways to enhance team performance through innovative tools and techniques. Leaders embarking on this journey are not just navigating the present; they are shaping a future where remote teams thrive on collaboration, accountability, and shared success. Ready to lead this charge, the question now is not if but how swiftly you can integrate these insights to propel your team toward unparalleled achievements?

11

Implementing Remote Performance Evaluation Systems

"Feedback is the breakfast of champions."
— Ken Blanchard

In the digital era, where teams are dispersed across the globe, the significance of implementing remote performance evaluation systems cannot be overstated. These systems serve as a linchpin for gauging individual and collective contributions, steering continuous development, and ensuring alignment with the broader organizational goals. This chapter embarks on a comprehensive exploration of the intricacies involved in establishing performance evaluation mechanisms that are not only effective but also equitable, fostering a culture where feedback drives growth and innovation.

The transition to remote work amplifies the need for clear, measurable, and transparent evaluation criteria that resonate with the distributed nature of teams. Entrepreneurs are tasked with the challenge of crafting evaluation systems that overcome geographical and temporal barriers, ensuring that every team member receives fair assessments that reflect their true contributions. By delineating best practices for leveraging technology, setting evaluation standards, and fostering a feedback-rich environment, this chapter offers a blueprint for entrepreneurs to navigate the complexities of remote performance evaluations.

At the heart of effective remote performance evaluations lies the dual objective of acknowledging achievements and identifying areas for growth. Entrepreneurs must ensure that these systems are imbued with a sense of fairness and objectivity, minimizing biases and fostering an environment where constructive feedback paves the way for continuous improvement. Through strategic planning, thoughtful implementation, and an unwavering commitment to development, leaders can harness the full potential of their distributed teams, driving success across the digital landscape.

Developing an effective remote performance evaluation system requires a nuanced understanding of the distributed workforce's unique dynamics. Entrepreneurs should focus on defining clear, relevant evaluation criteria that align with organizational objectives, ensuring that these metrics are communicated effectively across the team.

Technology plays a critical role in facilitating remote evaluations, offering platforms that can automate data collection, enable real-time feedback, and support virtual evaluation meetings. The selection of tools like performance management software, digital survey platforms, and video conferencing tools is crucial for conducting thorough and engaging performance discussions.

Opening Anecdote: GitLab's Transparent Evaluations

GitLab exemplifies the power of transparent and inclusive remote performance evaluation systems. Through an asynchronous process that emphasizes self-documentation of achievements and challenges, GitLab cultivates a culture where feedback is not just a formality but a cornerstone of team development and collaboration. Their approach, centered on clear KPIs and continuous feedback, demonstrates how remote evaluations can enhance performance and foster a culture of high achievement and mutual respect.

> **Quick Thought:**
> *A robust remote performance evaluation system transforms feedback into a strategic asset, enabling teams to navigate the complexities of remote work with clarity, purpose, and a focus on continuous growth.*

Entrepreneurship in Action: Key Ingredients

- **Objective Evaluation Criteria:** Establish and communicate clear, measurable criteria for evaluating performance, tailored to the unique aspects of remote work.
- **Consistent Evaluation Processes:** Implement structured processes for evaluations, incorporating self-assessments, peer feedback, and managerial reviews to foster a comprehensive understanding of performance.
- **Leverage of Technology:** Utilize specialized software and digital tools to streamline the evaluation process,

ensuring transparency, fairness, and accessibility for all team members.

Case Study: Upwork's Evaluation Innovation

Upwork, a leading platform for freelancers and remote work, has revolutionized the way performance evaluations are conducted in a distributed setting. By leveraging its unique position at the intersection of technology and global talent, Upwork has implemented a performance evaluation system that emphasizes flexibility, continuous feedback, and transparency. This system not only facilitates the professional growth of its vast network of freelancers but also ensures clients receive top-notch service, aligning individual achievements with broader business goals.

Flexible and Continuous Feedback Mechanism: Understanding the dynamic nature of freelance work, Upwork has designed a feedback mechanism that allows for continuous evaluation. This approach caters to the ebb and flow of project-based work, enabling freelancers to receive timely and relevant feedback that reflects their current performance. Clients are encouraged to provide reviews at the end of each project, contributing to a freelancer's overall rating and visibility on the platform.

Transparent Evaluation Criteria: Upwork's evaluation system is grounded in transparency. Freelancers and clients alike have clear visibility into the criteria used for performance assessments, including quality of work, adherence to deadlines, communication, and collaboration. This clarity fosters a sense of trust and accountability, encouraging both parties to engage in open and constructive dialogue about performance and expectations.

Technology-Driven Insights: At the core of Upwork's performance evaluation system is the strategic use of technology to gather and analyze data. The platform's algorithms consider various metrics, such as project completion rates, client satisfaction scores, and response times, to create comprehensive profiles of freelancers. These profiles help clients make informed hiring decisions and enable freelancers to understand their strengths and areas for improvement.

Empowerment through Professional Development: Recognizing the importance of continuous learning, Upwork offers resources and tools for freelancers to enhance their skills and competencies. From Upwork Academy to various skill certifications, these opportunities are integrated into the platform, allowing freelancers to directly link their learning achievements to their profiles, thereby influencing their performance evaluations positively.

Upwork's approach to remote performance evaluation exemplifies how technology can be harnessed to support the growth and development of a global workforce. By prioritizing flexibility, transparency, and continuous feedback, Upwork not only enhances the productivity and satisfaction of freelancers but also ensures clients have access to a pool of highly skilled professionals. This case study serves as an inspiration for leaders seeking to implement or refine remote performance evaluation systems, offering a blueprint for creating an environment that values continuous improvement and open communication.

```
Pro Tip:
Balance quantitative metrics with qualitative
feedback to paint a holistic picture of performance,
acknowledging not just what is achieved but also how
it is achieved.
```

Exercise: Remote Evaluation Mastery

Framework Development:

- **Remote Evaluation Strategy Session:** Host an interactive virtual workshop where leaders and team members collaborate to develop a comprehensive strategy for remote performance evaluations. This session will focus on identifying key performance indicators (KPIs), setting clear objectives, and outlining the evaluation process, ensuring alignment with organizational goals and remote work dynamics.
- **Criteria Crafting Seminar:** Lead a seminar dedicated to crafting detailed evaluation criteria that are both measurable and relevant to remote work contexts. Encourage participants to contribute insights from their experiences, fostering buy-in and ensuring that the criteria are inclusive and equitable.

Technology Integration:

- **Digital Tools Demo Day:** Organize a day where various performance management and feedback tools are demonstrated to the team. Allow team members to explore these tools in breakout sessions, providing hands-on experience and gathering input on which platforms best meet the team's needs.

- **Feedback System Workshop:** Conduct a practical workshop on setting up and using chosen digital platforms for remote evaluations. Include training on features that support continuous feedback, goal tracking, and performance reviews, ensuring that all team members are proficient in using the system.

Cultivating a Feedback Culture:

- **Feedback Training Series:** Implement a series of training sessions focused on effective feedback techniques in a remote setting. Cover topics such as giving constructive feedback, receiving feedback gracefully, and using feedback for professional development.
- **360-Degree Feedback Exercise:** Facilitate a 360-degree feedback cycle, guiding participants through the process of giving and receiving feedback from peers, subordinates, and supervisors. Use this exercise to highlight the value of diverse perspectives in performance assessments.

Challenge for You:

Implement a holistic remote performance evaluation system within your organization, incorporating elements from Framework Development, Technology Integration, and Cultivating a Feedback Culture. Over the next six months, monitor its effectiveness in enhancing transparency, fairness, and growth. Gather and integrate feedback from your team to refine the system, aiming for a process that not only evaluates performance but also fosters continuous professional development and team cohesion.

Concluding Thoughts:

Embracing the challenge of implementing remote performance evaluation systems marks a significant stride towards realizing the full potential of distributed teams. As we've navigated the complexities of creating fair, transparent, and effective evaluation mechanisms, it's evident that success hinges on empathy, strategic use of technology, and a steadfast commitment to a culture of continuous improvement. This journey, while intricate, offers a golden opportunity to redefine performance management in a way that not only measures success but actively contributes to it by empowering team members to achieve and surpass their goals. Leaders poised to embark on this transformative path will find themselves at the vanguard of cultivating resilient, high-performing teams adept at navigating the digital era's myriad challenges and opportunities. Are you ready to lead your team with insight and innovation, ensuring feedback becomes the cornerstone of professional growth and collective excellence?

12

Promoting Accountability and Measuring Results

"Accountability breeds response-ability."
— Stephen R. Covey

In the expansive world of remote work, the principles of accountability and precise measurement stand as critical pillars for team success. This chapter delves into the nuanced strategies required to instill a strong sense of responsibility among team members scattered across the globe and the mechanisms to accurately gauge their contributions. By weaving a culture of accountability into the fabric of remote teams, entrepreneurs lay the foundation for a disciplined, transparent, and high-performing work environment.

The shift to distributed teams brings with it the challenge of ensuring that every member remains aligned with the team's goals, motivated by their responsibilities, and cognizant of the impact of their work. Establishing clear expectations, paired with effective communication and feedback loops, becomes paramount in this context. This chapter presents actionable strategies for setting SMART goals, employing technology for performance tracking, and creating an environment where accountability is not just expected but celebrated. Through this, entrepreneurs can ensure that their teams not only meet but exceed the set benchmarks, driving the organization towards its broader objectives.

Yet, accountability extends beyond task completion; it encompasses the growth and development of each team member. By implementing robust measurement systems and fostering a culture where feedback is constructive and regular, leaders can guide their teams through continuous improvement. This chapter outlines how to leverage data-driven insights for performance assessment, the importance of recognizing achievements, and the ways to tailor rewards to individual and team successes. Through these efforts, entrepreneurs can cultivate a remote workforce that is not only accountable but also deeply engaged and committed to collective and personal excellence.

Promoting accountability in a distributed team requires a multifaceted approach that begins with setting clear, measurable goals. Entrepreneurs must ensure that these goals are well-communicated and understood by all team members, establishing a common ground for expectations and performance.

The use of performance management software and collaboration tools becomes indispensable in tracking progress and facilitating feedback. These technologies offer a transparent view of each team member's contributions and progress, allowing for timely interventions and acknowledgments.

Opening Anecdote: The LEGO Group's Building Blocks of Accountability

The LEGO Group, celebrated for bringing creative play into homes worldwide, extends its philosophy of innovation and meticulous design into promoting accountability within its remote teams. Through the implementation of a dynamic system that visually tracks progress and milestones, akin to assembling a LEGO set, the company fosters a culture where accountability is both a personal commitment and a collective mission. This visual and engaging approach ensures that each team member, no matter where they are located, plays a crucial part in constructing the company's success story, brick by brick.

> ### *Quick Thought:*
> *True accountability in remote teams is a symphony of clear expectations, open communication, and mutual trust, orchestrated through the thoughtful use of technology and feedback.*

Entrepreneurship in Action: Key Ingredients

- **Defining Clear Role Expectations:** Ensure that every team member knows what is expected of them and how their work contributes to the team's and organization's goals.
- **Implementing Robust Measurement Systems:** Use KPIs and performance data to objectively assess progress and outcomes, fostering a culture where results are trans-

parent and celebrated.

- **Fostering Open Communication:** Maintain regular communication channels for feedback, discussions, and acknowledgments, ensuring that team members feel valued and understood.

Case Study: Red Hat's Open Accountability Framework

Red Hat, a leading provider of open-source software solutions, has set a benchmark in fostering accountability and measuring results in a distributed environment. At the heart of Red Hat's culture lies a commitment to open source principles, not just in their products but also in their approach to team management and performance evaluation.

Cultivating a Culture of Openness and Responsibility: Red Hat's philosophy of open accountability is rooted in transparency, collaboration, and empowerment. By encouraging an environment where team members are open about their work, challenges, and achievements, Red Hat ensures that accountability is woven into the fabric of its corporate culture. This openness fosters a sense of ownership among employees, driving them to take responsibility for their contributions and their impact on the company's success.

Strategic Use of Performance Tracking Tools: Leveraging technology to enhance accountability, Red Hat employs a variety of tools designed to track progress, facilitate feedback, and celebrate achievements. Platforms such as Jira for project management and GitHub for code repository management enable team members to document their work, set milestones, and measure their results against clearly defined objectives.

These tools not only provide visibility into each team member's contributions but also facilitate a seamless flow of feedback, essential for continuous improvement and professional growth.

Empowering Teams through Autonomy and Clear Expectations: At Red Hat, accountability is paired with autonomy. Team members are empowered to manage their projects, make decisions, and take actions that align with the company's strategic goals. This empowerment is balanced with clear expectations – set through the collaborative establishment of Objectives and Key Results (OKRs) – ensuring that individual efforts contribute to the broader organizational objectives. Red Hat's leadership emphasizes the importance of setting realistic, measurable goals that challenge and motivate team members, fostering a results-oriented mindset across the organization.

Fostering Continuous Improvement through Constructive Feedback: A cornerstone of Red Hat's approach to accountability is its emphasis on regular, constructive feedback. Performance reviews are not confined to annual assessments but are part of an ongoing dialogue between team members and their managers. This continuous feedback loop, supported by regular one-on-one meetings and team retrospectives, ensures that performance management is a dynamic, integral part of the work process, allowing for real-time adjustments and fostering a culture of continuous learning and development.

Recognition and Rewarding Excellence: Recognizing and rewarding achievements plays a pivotal role in Red Hat's accountability framework. The company has instituted various recognition programs that highlight individual and team successes, linking them to the company's values and objectives. These programs not only celebrate achievements but also reinforce the behaviors and outcomes that Red Hat aims to promote, further embedding accountability into the organizational ethos.

Red Hat's open accountability framework demonstrates how a culture of transparency, empowerment, and continuous feedback can drive a distributed team to achieve exceptional results. By aligning technology, clear expectations, and a supportive feedback mechanism with the company's core values, Red Hat has created a dynamic and inclusive work environment where accountability is a shared responsibility, propelling the organization towards its strategic goals.

```
Pro Tip:
Encourage team members to share their progress and
challenges openly in regular team meetings or
through digital platforms, fostering a culture where
accountability is paired with support and
collaboration.
```

Exercise: Accountability and Results Mastery

Strategic Alignment:

- **Interactive Goal-Setting Workshop:** Facilitate an engaging online workshop where team members and leaders collaboratively establish SMART (Specific, Measurable, Achievable, Relevant, Time-bound) goals. This session aims to align individual objectives with the broader vision of the organization, ensuring clarity and shared purpose.

- **Role Clarity Session:** Organize a session dedicated to clarifying roles and responsibilities within the team. Utilize interactive tools to map out how each role contributes to the organization's goals, enhancing transparency and understanding.

Technology Empowerment:

- **Digital Performance Tracking Tutorial:** Conduct a comprehensive tutorial on utilizing selected performance tracking and management tools. Focus on features that allow for real-time progress monitoring, feedback sharing, and celebrating achievements, ensuring all team members are proficient in leveraging technology to foster accountability.
- **Feedback Platform Exploration:** Explore and implement a digital feedback platform, providing training for team members on giving and receiving constructive feedback. This platform should facilitate regular, transparent, and constructive communication, supporting a culture of continuous improvement.

Cultural Shift Toward Accountability:

- **Open Communication Workshop:** Host a workshop on fostering open and honest communication within remote teams. Include sessions on active listening, effective feedback techniques, and conflict resolution, aiming to build a supportive environment where accountability is seen as a path to growth.

- **Recognition and Rewards Brainstorm:** Facilitate a brainstorming session to develop innovative recognition and reward mechanisms that align with remote work dynamics. Encourage creativity in finding ways to celebrate individual and team successes, reinforcing the link between accountability and positive outcomes.

Challenge for You:

Commit to enhancing accountability within your distributed team by implementing a structured framework that includes strategic goal alignment, empowered use of technology, and a cultural shift towards open communication and recognition. Over the next six months, monitor the effectiveness of these initiatives in promoting a disciplined, transparent, and high-performing work environment. Adjust and refine your approach based on ongoing feedback and the evolving needs of your team.

Concluding Thoughts:

Cultivating accountability and precision in measuring results within a distributed environment represents the cornerstone of sustained team success and operational excellence. This chapter has illuminated the path towards establishing an ecosystem where responsibility is not just a mandate but a shared ethos, driving every team member towards collective and individual achievements. The integration of clear goals, transparent communication, and the strategic use of technology forms a robust framework that can significantly elevate a team's productivity and cohesion, regardless of the geographical distances that divide them. As we reflect on the strategies and insights shared, the question remains: Are you ready to harness the power of accountability and results-oriented practices to lead your remote team to new pinnacles of success?

13

Recognizing and Rewarding Remote Team Performance

"Appreciation is a wonderful thing: It makes what is excellent in
others belong to us as well."
— Voltaire

In the dispersed world of remote work, the art of recognizing and rewarding team performance becomes both a challenge and a critical driver of success. This chapter illuminates the path for entrepreneurs to celebrate achievements and foster a culture of appreciation that transcends digital boundaries. By crafting thoughtful recognition and reward programs, leaders can motivate their teams, boost morale, and cultivate a sense of belonging and achievement, ensuring that the remote work environment is vibrant, engaging, and productive.

The essence of effective recognition in a remote setting lies in understanding the unique dynamics of virtual teams and tailoring acknowledgment to meet those needs. It's about creating moments of connection that resonate deeply with team members, making them feel truly seen and valued for their contributions. This chapter delves into the strategies for delivering timely, meaningful, and diverse forms of recognition that align with individual preferences and reinforce the organization's values and goals. From public accolades to personalized gestures, the goal is to build a comprehensive approach that celebrates excellence in a manner that motivates and resonates with each remote team member.

Moreover, the chapter explores the symbiotic relationship between recognition and rewards, highlighting how they serve not just as a tool for affirmation but as a mechanism for furthering engagement and driving performance. Through real-world examples and practical insights, entrepreneurs are guided on designing and implementing reward systems that are both aspirational and attainable, fostering an environment where excellence is not only recognized but also aspired to. By integrating these elements into the remote work culture, leaders can ensure that their teams are not only aligned with but also deeply invested in the collective success of the organization.

To foster a genuine culture of recognition, it's crucial to establish clear and transparent criteria that guide how achievements are acknowledged. Entrepreneurs should ensure these criteria are closely tied to the company's core values and objectives, making the recognition meaningful and aligned with broader goals.

Implementing a variety of recognition methods caters to the diverse preferences within a remote team. From digital shout-outs to virtual awards ceremonies, the key is to keep the recognition fresh, personal, and reflective of each team member's unique contribution.

Opening Anecdote: The Virgin Group's Celebration of Stars

The Virgin Group, with its diverse portfolio of businesses, thrives on recognizing and rewarding the performance of its remote teams through innovative and heartfelt initiatives. Richard Branson's ethos of employee appreciation manifests in the group's "Celebration of Stars" program, which empowers employees to nominate peers who exemplify the Virgin spirit— innovation, customer service, and a bit of fun. These stories of excellence are shared across global platforms, creating a ripple effect of motivation and fostering a culture where every contribution is acknowledged and celebrated, making every team member feel like a star in the Virgin galaxy.

> **Quick Thought:**
> *Recognition in remote teams should be as much about the message as the medium, ensuring that every gesture of appreciation bridges the digital divide and touches the hearts of team members.*

Entrepreneurship in Action: Key Ingredients

- **Diverse Recognition Methods:** Adapt recognition practices to suit the digital realm, ensuring they are personal, timely, and reflective of individual achievements and contributions.
- **Transparent Reward Systems:** Build reward systems

that are clear, fair, and directly tied to recognizable and measurable outcomes, promoting a culture of meritocracy.

- **Continuous Feedback Loop:** Incorporate recognition into the regular feedback and communication channels to keep motivation and engagement levels high.

Case Study: Assembla's Culture of Recognition and Excellence

Assembla, a cloud-based version control and source code management service, is distinguished for its unique approach to recognizing and rewarding the performance of its remote team. The company's innovative "Shout Outs" initiative, a peer-to-peer recognition system, underscores the effectiveness of empowering employees to acknowledge each other's contributions. This not only enhances individual morale but also fortifies the collective team spirit, creating a work environment where excellence is continuously celebrated and motivation is consistently high.

Cultivating a Recognition-Rich Environment: At Assembla, the culture of recognition is deeply embedded into daily operations. The "Shout Outs" program is designed to be inclusive and transparent, allowing team members to publicly acknowledge their peers for achievements that contribute to the company's goals and values. This approach leverages the diversity of the team, ensuring that recognition is reflective of the broad spectrum of contributions that fuel the company's success.

Leveraging Technology for Meaningful Acknowledgment: Assembla utilizes its digital platforms to facilitate this recognition, ensuring that shout outs are visible and celebrated across the organization. This visibility not only amplifies the sense of achievement for the individual being recognized but also serves as a powerful motivator for the entire team. By making these acknowledgments public, Assembla reinforces the behaviors and outcomes it seeks to promote, further embedding its core values into its team culture.

Balancing Public Praise with Personalized Rewards: In addition to public recognition, Assembla understands the importance of personalizing rewards to match the individual preferences and contributions of its team members. Whether through professional development opportunities, flexible working arrangements, or other tailored rewards, Assembla ensures that its appreciation resonates on a personal level, enhancing the impact of its recognition efforts.

Continuous Feedback and Recognition Integration: Assembla's recognition strategy is complemented by a continuous feedback mechanism, where constructive feedback and accolades go hand in hand. This balance fosters a culture where team members are not only driven by the prospect of recognition but are also committed to ongoing personal and professional growth.

Assembla's approach to recognizing and rewarding remote team performance illustrates a profound understanding of the dynamics of distributed work environments. By creating a transparent, inclusive, and supportive recognition culture, Assembla not only boosts team morale and engagement but also sets a standard for how remote teams can cultivate a sense of belonging and achievement. This case study serves as an inspiration for leaders looking to harness the power of recognition to drive their remote teams towards greater cohesion, productivity, and excellence.

Pro Tip:
Leverage technology to create a centralized
recognition platform where achievements are
continuously celebrated, making recognition a
dynamic and integral part of the company culture.

Exercise: Excellence Recognition and Reward

Establishing Recognition Foundations:

- **Values-Aligned Recognition Workshop:** Conduct an interactive session to establish recognition practices that reflect the company's core values and objectives. This workshop encourages leaders and team members to identify behaviors and achievements that exemplify these values, creating a direct link between recognition and the organization's mission.
- **Diversity in Recognition Methods:** Host a brainstorming session to explore diverse and creative ways to recognize team members in a remote setting. Emphasize personalization and inclusivity, ensuring that the methods resonate with the varied cultural and personal backgrounds of the team.

Enhancing Reward Systems:

- **Transparent Rewards Framework Session:** Design a

clear and equitable rewards system that is well-understood by all team members. Discuss the balance between tangible rewards and intrinsic motivators, aligning them with the recognition criteria established.

- **Reward Personalization Workshop:** Create a platform for team members to express what types of rewards are most meaningful to them. Use this feedback to tailor rewards, making them more impactful and motivational.

Building a Culture of Continuous Recognition:

- **Integrated Feedback and Recognition Systems:** Develop a continuous feedback loop that incorporates regular recognition moments. Use digital tools to facilitate ongoing acknowledgment of small wins and significant achievements, reinforcing a culture of appreciation.
- **Public Recognition Practices:** Implement a series of public recognition practices, such as "Employee of the Month" showcased on company-wide channels or special acknowledgments during virtual team meetings. These practices should celebrate both individual contributions and team successes.

Challenge for You:

Initiate a recognition and reward pilot program based on the strategies developed during the workshop. Over the next three months, actively apply these strategies, seeking to cover a broad spectrum of recognition and reward types. Monitor the program's impact on team engagement, morale, and overall performance. Gather team feedback to refine and expand the program, aiming to embed recognition deeply into your remote work culture.

Concluding Thoughts:

The journey of embedding recognition and rewarding excellence within a remote team is transformative, offering a beacon for navigating the challenges of distance with the light of appreciation and acknowledgement. This chapter has traversed the landscape of creating meaningful moments of recognition that transcend the digital divide, fostering a culture where every achievement, no matter how small, is celebrated. The strategies and insights shared underscore the importance of aligning recognition with organizational values, ensuring that every team member feels seen, valued, and motivated. As we reflect on the path to cultivating a vibrant, engaged, and productive remote work environment, the question remains: Are you ready to embrace the art of recognition, transforming your remote team into a cohesive unit where excellence is not just recognized but deeply celebrated?

14

Running Effective Virtual Meetings and Workshops

"The single biggest problem in communication is the illusion that it has taken place."
— George Bernard Shaw

I n the tapestry of remote work, virtual meetings and workshops are the threads that bind the fabric of teamwork and collaboration. This chapter embarks on a journey to refine these essential tools of digital interaction, ensuring they serve not merely as substitutes for in-person engagements but as powerful platforms for innovation, decision-making, and team bonding. By mastering the art of conducting effective virtual meetings and workshops, entrepreneurs can transcend geographical limitations, harnessing the full potential of their distributed teams.

The cornerstone of successful virtual gatherings lies in meticulous preparation and the deliberate crafting of agendas that promise clear objectives and meaningful engagement. Entrepreneurs face the challenge of navigating the digital divide, turning potential obstacles into opportunities for enhanced communication and collaboration. This chapter unfolds a series of strategies designed to elevate virtual meetings from routine check-ins to transformative sessions that energize teams, clarify goals, and foster a culture of accountability and shared success.

Beyond the technical execution, the essence of running impactful virtual meetings and workshops is found in the human touch—engaging each participant, acknowledging their contributions, and creating an inclusive environment that values every voice. Through practical guidance and best practices, this chapter provides entrepreneurs with the tools to facilitate discussions that not only reach decisions but also build connections, ensuring that every remote meeting becomes a stepping stone towards achieving collective and individual milestones.

Effective virtual meetings hinge on the dual pillars of robust preparation and dynamic facilitation. Entrepreneurs must navigate the selection of appropriate tools that not only facilitate seamless communication but also invite active participation and collaboration among team members.

Creating an environment conducive to productive and engaging virtual discussions requires a blend of clear communication, active listening, and time management skills. Facilitators must adeptly guide conversations, ensuring that objectives are met while fostering an atmosphere of inclusivity and mutual respect.

Opening Anecdote: Miro's Collaborative Planning Mastery

Miro, with its collaborative online whiteboard platform, epitomizes the seamless integration of preparation and engagement in virtual meetings. By leveraging their own tools to outline agendas collaboratively and visually engage participants, Miro sets a benchmark for how virtual spaces can be optimized for creativity, strategic planning, and team alignment. Their approach demonstrates that with the right preparation and tools, virtual meetings can become crucibles of collaboration and innovation.

> **Quick Thought:**
> *The true measure of effective virtual meetings lies not in the technology employed but in the connections forged and the decisions reached, transforming digital interactions into meaningful outcomes.*

Entrepreneurship in Action: Key Ingredients

- **Purpose-Driven Agendas:** Craft agendas with clear objectives and outcomes, ensuring every virtual meeting has a defined purpose that aligns with broader team goals.
- **Participant Engagement:** Deploy interactive tools and techniques to maintain high levels of engagement, ensuring every team member has a voice and contributes to the discussion.
- **Effective Facilitation:** Embrace the role of facilitator with a focus on clear communication, active listening, and

adept time management to drive productive discussions and outcomes.

Case Study: Monday.com's Empowerment Through Engagement

Monday.com, a leader in project management solutions, sets a compelling example of how to run effective virtual meetings and workshops that drive engagement, clarity, and strategic alignment. By integrating their platform's capabilities with a deep understanding of virtual collaboration dynamics, Monday.com creates an environment where every participant is not only heard but also empowered to contribute meaningfully to the team's objectives.

Cultivating a Culture of Engagement: At the core of Monday.com's approach is the belief that engagement is the cornerstone of productive virtual meetings. Through the use of their project management platform, the company ensures that each meeting is meticulously prepared, with clear agendas that outline objectives, expected outcomes, and roles for each participant. This level of preparation ensures that meetings are focused and purpose-driven, maximizing the use of time and keeping participants engaged throughout.

Leveraging Technology for Interactive Meetings: Monday.com leverages its software to enhance interaction during meetings, employing features such as live polling, task assignments, and progress tracking in real-time. These features not only facilitate a more dynamic meeting experience but also ensure that decisions and actions are immediately integrated into the team's workflow, promoting accountability and transparency.

Facilitation Techniques that Foster Inclusivity: Understanding that effective facilitation is key to engaging virtual meetings, Monday.com trains its leaders and team facilitators in communication techniques that promote inclusivity. This includes active listening, encouraging participation from all members, and using breakout sessions for brainstorming or tackling complex issues in smaller groups. By doing so, Monday.com ensures that its virtual meetings are spaces where diverse ideas are explored and every voice is valued.

Recognition and Follow-up for Sustained Engagement: Post-meeting follow-ups are an integral part of Monday.com's strategy. The company utilizes its platform to send summaries, assign action items, and solicit feedback on the meeting's effectiveness. This not only reinforces the meeting's outcomes but also demonstrates appreciation for each participant's contributions, further fostering a culture of engagement and continuous improvement.

Monday.com's strategy for running effective virtual meetings and workshops exemplifies how preparation, technology, and skilled facilitation come together to create engaging and productive digital workspaces. Their success in maintaining high levels of team engagement across a distributed workforce highlights the potential for virtual meetings to not just replicate but enhance the collaborative experience, driving team cohesion and performance. Assembla and other organizations looking to elevate their virtual collaboration practices can draw valuable lessons from Monday.com's approach, recognizing that the key to effective virtual meetings lies in the deliberate fusion of technology, inclusivity, and empowerment.

```
Pro Tip:
Utilize breakout rooms for focused discussions or
brainstorming sessions within larger meetings to
encourage deeper collaboration and ensure that every
participant has the opportunity to contribute.
```

Exercise: Advanced Virtual Meeting Facilitation

Structuring Engaging Agendas:

- **Purpose-Driven Agenda Crafting Session:** Dive into crafting engaging agendas that align with the meeting's objectives, focusing on including elements that foster interaction and decision-making. This session will guide participants through the process of constructing agendas that ensure productive and goal-oriented meetings.
- **Interactive Techniques Lab:** Explore and practice various interactive techniques to enhance engagement in virtual meetings. From live polls and quizzes to collaborative document editing, discover how to integrate these tools seamlessly into your meetings to keep participants engaged and invested.

Facilitation Skills Enhancement:

- **Dynamic Facilitation Workshop:** Engage in a hands-on workshop aimed at enhancing facilitation skills for virtual settings. Focus on techniques for effective communication, managing diverse viewpoints, and keeping discussions on track, all while fostering an inclusive atmosphere that encourages every participant to contribute.

- **Breakout Room Strategy Session:** Learn how to effectively use breakout rooms for smaller group discussions or brainstorming sessions within larger meetings. This includes strategies for setting up, monitoring, and integrating breakout discussions back into the main meeting flow.

Challenge for You:

Over the next two months, commit to applying a new strategy or technique in each virtual meeting or workshop you conduct. Start with rethinking your agenda design to include more interactive elements and then move on to experimenting with advanced facilitation techniques, such as using breakout rooms for deep dives on specific topics. After each meeting, gather feedback from participants on the effectiveness of these strategies and their impact on engagement and productivity. Use this feedback to refine your approach, aiming to create a more dynamic, inclusive, and productive virtual meeting environment.

Concluding Thoughts:

The realm of virtual meetings and workshops represents more than just a necessity in the world of remote work; it's a fertile ground for innovation, connection, and collaborative success. As this chapter concludes, it beckons leaders to reevaluate and enrich their approach to digital gatherings, turning them into powerful conduits for strategic alignment, collective brainstorming, and the deepening of team bonds. The journey towards mastering virtual interactions is ongoing, demanding continuous learning, experimentation, and an unwavering commitment to elevating the virtual workspace. The question now is, are you prepared to harness the full potential of your virtual meetings and workshops, transforming them into key drivers of your team's success and cohesion?

15

Facilitating Productive Discussions and Decision-Making

"Good decisions come from experience, and experience comes from bad decisions."
— Mark Twain

In the realm of remote work, the capacity to facilitate productive discussions and steer decisive action is paramount. This chapter ventures into the art and science of orchestrating discussions that not only engage but also propel distributed teams toward consensus and action. Amid the digital expanse, the challenge for entrepreneurs lies in bridging physical distances to create a virtual space where ideas flourish, diverse viewpoints are celebrated, and decisions are made with clarity and conviction.

The foundation of fruitful virtual discussions rests on a bedrock of clear objectives, inclusive participation, and a steadfast commitment to understanding and leveraging the nuances of digital communication. By setting the stage with well-defined ground rules and a purpose-driven agenda, leaders can navigate the complexities of remote collaboration. This chapter unfolds the strategies to cultivate an environment where every team member feels heard, valued, and empowered to contribute, transforming the virtual meeting room into a crucible of creativity and strategic thinking.

Effective decision-making in a distributed setting demands a nuanced approach that respects the diversity of thought and experience within the team. Entrepreneurs are tasked with harnessing this diversity to forge decisions that are not only informed but also widely embraced. Through the lenses of inclusivity, active facilitation, and the judicious use of technology, this chapter guides leaders on a journey to master the delicate balance between guiding discussions and fostering a culture where decisions emerge organically from the collective intelligence of the team.

To navigate the intricacies of remote discussions and decision-making, leaders must become adept at fostering an environment that encourages open dialogue and mutual respect. Strategies such as actively soliciting diverse perspectives, employing interactive techniques to maintain engagement, and addressing conflicts with empathy and clarity become essential.

Technology plays a pivotal role in supporting these endeavors, offering platforms and tools that facilitate seamless interaction, idea sharing, and consensus-building. From utilizing breakout rooms for focused discussions to leveraging decision-making software for transparent and democratic processes, the digital landscape offers myriad opportunities to enhance the collaborative experience.

Opening Anecdote: Atlassian Confluence's Collaboration Mastery

Atlassian Confluence epitomizes the power of structured yet flexible virtual discussions in forging team unity and driving decision-making. By leveraging their platform to set clear agendas, share pre-meeting materials, and encourage active participation, Atlassian demonstrates that effective virtual collaboration is built on preparation, transparency, and a shared commitment to achieving goals. Their approach highlights how digital tools can be harnessed to facilitate discussions that are both productive and inclusive.

> **Quick Thought:**
> *The success of virtual discussions and decision-making hinges on a leader's ability to blend strategic planning with empathetic facilitation, ensuring every voice is heard and every decision is a step toward shared objectives.*

Entrepreneurship in Action: Key Ingredients

- **Inclusive Environment:** Cultivate a space where diverse perspectives are not just welcomed but actively sought, recognizing the value of varied experiences in enriching discussions and informing decisions.
- **Structured Flexibility:** Balance the need for structured agendas with the flexibility to explore ideas, pivot discussions as needed, and adapt to the team's dynamic needs.
- **Technological Leverage:** Harness the power of digital tools to break down barriers to participation, enhance

117

communication, and streamline the decision-making process.

Case Study: Canva's Collaborative Design Revolution

Background: Melanie Perkins, the co-founder and CEO of Canva, revolutionized the graphic design industry with an intuitive, user-friendly platform that democratized design for professionals and non-designers alike. Canva's inception was rooted in Perkins's vision to simplify the design process, making it accessible to everyone, everywhere. This ambition led to the creation of a platform that supports real-time collaboration across global teams, embodying the essence of innovation and continuous learning in the digital workspace.

Fostering a Culture of Innovation and Collaboration: At the heart of Canva's success is a company culture that champions creativity, experimentation, and a relentless pursuit of excellence. Perkins has cultivated an environment where team members are encouraged to propose ideas, test new concepts, and learn from both successes and failures. This culture of open innovation has propelled Canva into a leading position in the online design space, with millions of users worldwide leveraging the platform to bring their creative projects to life.

Embracing Global Team Dynamics: Canva's distributed team model showcases effective management of remote dynamics, with staff located around the globe collaborating seamlessly. Perkins's leadership style—emphasizing empathy, clear communication, and trust—has been pivotal in building a cohesive and resilient team. Canva utilizes a suite of digital collaboration tools to ensure that regardless of location, all team members have a voice and can contribute to the platform's continuous development.

Continuous Learning and User-Centered Innovation: Central to Canva's ethos is a commitment to continuous improvement and user-centered design. Perkins leads by example, fostering a learning environment where feedback from users and team members alike drives the platform's evolution. This approach has enabled Canva to stay at the forefront of technological advancements and user experience design, continually adding new features and capabilities in response to user needs.

Impact and Expansion: Canva's journey from a start-up idea to a multi-billion-dollar company is a testament to the power of visionary leadership in the digital age. Under Perkins's stewardship, Canva has not only transformed the design industry but also created a global community of designers, educators, and entrepreneurs who share a common goal of bringing their ideas to life through visual content.

Melanie Perkins's leadership at Canva exemplifies the transformative impact of embracing innovation, fostering a culture of continuous learning, and effectively managing a distributed team. By prioritizing user experience, promoting a collaborative work environment, and leveraging technology to connect a global team, Canva has set a new standard for digital-age companies. Perkins's journey provides invaluable lessons on the potential for digital tools to unite teams around the world in the pursuit of collective creativity and innovation.

```
Pro Tip:
Embrace the "parking lot" concept during discussions
to acknowledge off-topic but valuable ideas,
ensuring they are revisited without derailing the
immediate agenda.
```

Exercise: Dynamic Decision-Making and Discussion Facilitation

Objective-Driven Planning:

- **Purposeful Agenda Crafting Session:** Learn how to design agendas that ensure each meeting is purpose-driven and aligned with team objectives. This interactive session guides participants through structuring agendas to maximize engagement and productivity, with a focus on clear outcomes.

- **Engagement Strategy Lab:** Explore innovative strategies to engage every participant in virtual discussions, using techniques such as polling, interactive Q&A sessions, and collaborative document editing to foster a lively and inclusive meeting environment.

Inclusive Discussion Techniques:

- **Diverse Perspectives Roundtable:** Conduct a simulated meeting aiming to draw out diverse viewpoints, focusing on techniques for encouraging silent participants and managing dominant voices to ensure a balanced and inclusive discussion.

- **Conflict Resolution Workshop:** Learn to navigate and resolve conflicts in virtual discussions with empathy, maintaining a positive and constructive environment. Practice strategies for addressing disagreements and turning them into opportunities for deeper understanding and team cohesion.

Challenge for You:

Over the next three months, commit to implementing at least one new discussion or decision-making technique in your virtual meetings. Begin with integrating more structured yet flexible agendas to foster purposeful discussions and gradually introduce methods for enhancing participant engagement and inclusivity. After each meeting, solicit feedback from team members on the effectiveness of these new approaches and their impact on the discussion's productivity and decision-making quality. Use this feedback to refine your facilitation style, aiming to create more dynamic, inclusive, and effective virtual meeting experiences.

Concluding Thoughts:

Embarking on the journey to refine virtual discussions and decision-making processes is essential in today's digital workspace. This chapter has armed you with strategies and insights to transform virtual meetings from mere check-ins into powerful platforms for collaborative success. The challenge now is to apply these learnings, embracing the nuances of digital communication to foster an environment where every team member can contribute their best. With the right mix of technology, empathy, and strategic facilitation, you can steer your team towards making informed decisions that propel your organization forward. Are you ready to elevate your leadership and drive your remote team towards unparalleled success and consensus?

16

Managing Conflict and Resolving Issues Remotely

"Peace is not absence of conflict, it is the ability to handle conflict by peaceful means."
— Ronald Reagan

In the intricate web of remote work, managing conflict and resolving issues stands as a pivotal challenge for leaders. This chapter dives deep into the art of navigating these waters in distributed teams, where the absence of face-to-face interactions demands an even greater emphasis on communication skills, understanding, and empathy. It underscores the importance of recognizing the unique challenges that arise in virtual settings and offers a roadmap for turning potential discord into opportunities for growth and unity.

At the heart of effective conflict resolution is the leader's ability to foster an environment where open dialogue, cultural sensitivity, and constructive feedback are the norms. This chapter presents strategies for preempting conflicts through clear expectations and robust communication channels and for resolving them through active listening and empathetic engagement. By embracing these practices, entrepreneurs can cultivate a culture of transparency and trust, ensuring their teams remain cohesive and focused on their collective goals.

The resolution of conflicts in a distributed team not only tests the resilience and adaptability of its members but also strengthens the fabric of the team itself. Through a combination of proactive measures and responsive strategies, leaders can guide their teams through disagreements and challenges, emerging stronger on the other side. This chapter provides the tools for entrepreneurs to master the delicate balance of addressing conflicts head-on while maintaining harmony and productivity across geographies.

Effective conflict management in remote settings requires a nuanced approach that accounts for the complexities of digital communication and cultural diversity. Entrepreneurs must navigate these challenges with a blend of proactive planning, skilled facilitation, and an unwavering commitment to fostering an inclusive and respectful work environment.

Technology plays a crucial role in facilitating conflict resolution remotely, offering platforms that support real-time communication, visual cues, and collaborative problem-solving. By leveraging these digital tools, leaders can create a space where issues are addressed promptly and effectively, ensuring the team's momentum is maintained.

Opening Anecdote: The IKEA Approach to Harmony

IKEA, a brand synonymous with making homes harmonious, applies the same principle to managing conflicts within its remote teams. By adopting a proactive approach grounded in empathy, clear communication, and mutual respect, IKEA sets the stage for constructive dialogue and effective resolution. Their virtual conflict resolution workshops, inspired by the simplicity and functionality of their products, serve as a model for turning potential discord into harmony, ensuring the team's fabric remains intact and stronger than ever.

> **Quick Thought:**
> *Conflict, when managed effectively, can be a catalyst for innovation and team growth, transforming challenges into opportunities for strengthening trust and collaboration.*

Entrepreneurship in Action: Key Ingredients

- **Cultural Sensitivity:** Cultivate an environment where cultural diversity is celebrated, and all team members feel respected and understood.
- **Proactive Communication:** Implement clear communication channels and encourage open dialogue to prevent misunderstandings and swiftly address emerging conflicts.
- **Empathetic Resolution:** Approach conflict resolution with empathy and active listening, ensuring all parties feel heard and valued in finding a mutual solution.

Case Study: Zoho's Culture of Open Dialogue and Resolution

Zoho's approach to managing conflict and resolving issues remotely showcases the company's dedication to maintaining a positive and transparent team culture. Recognized for its suite of online productivity tools and SaaS applications, Zoho understands the complexities of remote work and the importance of addressing conflicts in a distributed team environment.

Proactive Conflict Management: Zoho stands out for its proactive stance on conflict management. The company fosters an environment where open dialogue is encouraged, and conflicts are seen as opportunities for growth rather than obstacles. By embedding cultural sensitivity and proactive communication into the core of its operations, Zoho minimizes the potential for misunderstandings that could lead to conflict. This preventative strategy is underpinned by regular training sessions on effective communication, cultural diversity, and emotional intelligence, equipping team members with the skills needed to navigate the nuances of remote interactions.

Technology-Enhanced Resolution Processes: Leveraging its technological expertise, Zoho utilizes a variety of digital tools to facilitate conflict resolution. Platforms like Zoho Connect and Zoho Cliq are not just used for day-to-day communications but also serve as vital channels for addressing and resolving issues. Video conferencing features are employed to ensure that discussions about sensitive issues have a personal touch, while shared online documents and whiteboards are used to collaboratively work through problems and document resolutions.

Empathetic and Solution-Focused Approach: Central to Zoho's conflict resolution strategy is an empathetic and solution-focused approach. Leaders and managers are trained to listen actively and empathetically, acknowledging the perspectives and feelings of all parties involved. This fosters a sense of being heard and valued, crucial in remote settings where non-verbal cues are absent. Furthermore, Zoho emphasizes finding collaborative solutions, encouraging team members to engage in constructive dialogue and brainstorming sessions to resolve conflicts with mutually beneficial outcomes.

Cultural Initiatives for Team Cohesion: Beyond immediate conflict resolution, Zoho invests in long-term cultural initiatives that build team cohesion and prevent future conflicts. These include virtual team-building activities, cross-cultural exchange programs, and regular "Ask Me Anything" sessions with leadership. Such initiatives not only enhance understanding and empathy among team members but also reinforce a culture where conflicts are addressed openly and respectfully.

Zoho's methodical and empathetic approach to conflict resolution in a remote work environment highlights the importance of a strong team culture, the strategic use of technology, and the value of empathy and collaboration. By prioritizing open communication, proactive conflict prevention, and inclusive problem-solving, Zoho successfully navigates the challenges of remote work, turning potential conflicts into opportunities for strengthening team bonds and enhancing overall performance. Other organizations looking to improve their remote conflict resolution strategies can learn from Zoho's example, recognizing that the foundation of effective conflict management lies in fostering an environment of transparency, respect, and collective problem-solving.

```
Pro Tip:
Utilize virtual conflict resolution tools to enhance
dialogue and understanding among team members,
making use of features like video conferencing for a
more personal touch and shared documents for clarity
and transparency.
```

Exercise: Remote Conflict Resolution Mastery

Understanding and Preparation:

- **Conflict Awareness Session:** Dive into the common sources of conflict in remote teams, from misunderstandings due to lack of non-verbal cues to clashes arising from cultural differences. This session helps in recognizing early signs of conflict and understanding its potential impact on team dynamics.
- **Preventive Strategies Lab:** Explore proactive communication strategies and setting clear expectations to prevent conflicts. Participants will learn how to establish a team charter that includes conflict resolution protocols, enhancing the team's resilience against potential disagreements.

Active Resolution Techniques:

- **Empathetic Listening Exercises:** Practice the skill of empathetic listening through role-play scenarios that mirror real-life conflicts. Learn to navigate conversations with a focus on understanding and validating team members' perspectives before moving towards resolution.
- **Solution-Focused Mediation Workshop:** Gain hands-on experience in mediating conflicts with a solution-focused approach. Participants will be guided through the steps of neutral facilitation, encouraging open dialogue and collaborative problem-solving among conflicting parties.

Challenge for You:

Over the next three months, proactively apply at least two conflict resolution strategies or practices from this workshop in real-world scenarios within your team. Start with preventive measures, such as improving communication protocols or conducting a cultural sensitivity session. Should conflicts arise, employ empathetic listening and solution-focused mediation techniques to address and resolve these issues. Document each conflict situation, your approach to resolution, and the outcomes, reflecting on the effectiveness of the strategies used and areas for improvement. This ongoing exercise aims to enhance your competency in managing and resolving conflicts remotely, contributing to a more cohesive and collaborative team environment.

Concluding Thoughts:

Stepping into the realm of remote leadership, the ability to manage conflict and foster resolution is not just a skill— it's a necessity for building strong, resilient teams. As we journey through the complexities of remote work, the insights from this chapter provide a robust framework for preempting, addressing, and resolving conflicts with grace and effectiveness. The strategies and tools outlined here are designed to empower you to create an environment of open communication, mutual respect, and empathetic engagement. As you apply these principles, remember that every conflict resolved strengthens the bonds of your team, turning potential obstacles into opportunities for growth and unity. Are you ready to embrace the challenges of conflict resolution as opportunities to reinforce the fabric of your remote team, leading them towards greater harmony and productivity?

17

Leveraging Technology for Remote Team Productivity

"Technology is best when it brings people together."
— Matt Mullenweg

In the tapestry of modern business, technology serves as both the thread and the loom, weaving together distributed teams across the globe. This chapter delves into the pivotal role technology plays in enhancing the productivity and cohesion of remote teams. By judiciously selecting and implementing a suite of digital tools, entrepreneurs can transcend geographical limitations, fostering a work environment that is both dynamic and efficient.

The landscape of remote work is replete with challenges, from communication barriers to project management hurdles. However, with the advent of sophisticated collaboration and productivity tools, entrepreneurs have at their disposal an arsenal to combat these challenges. This chapter outlines the essential technologies that can streamline workflows, enhance communication, and ensure seamless collaboration, thereby elevating team productivity to new heights.

The digital age demands a shift from conventional work paradigms to more agile and flexible models. Through the strategic application of technology, entrepreneurs can create a virtual workspace that mirrors the efficiency and connectivity of a physical office. This chapter provides a roadmap for harnessing the power of technology to not only maintain but also amplify team productivity in a remote setting.

In the realm of remote work, the selection of technology is not just about choosing tools, but about crafting an ecosystem that supports every facet of virtual teamwork. From communication platforms that bridge time zones to project management tools that visualize progress, the right technology stack can be the difference between a disorganized team and a synchronized unit.

Entrepreneurs must navigate the vast landscape of digital tools, identifying those that offer the best fit for their team's unique needs. This includes not only the functionality of the tools but also their interoperability, user-friendliness, and security features. The chapter explores criteria for selecting these tools and strategies for their effective implementation.

Opening Anecdote: The Philips Innovation Hub

Philips, a leader in health technology, has transformed remote work challenges into opportunities for innovation and productivity through its digital Innovation Hub. This virtual space not only facilitates project management and team collaboration across continents but also serves as a breeding ground for creative solutions, leveraging Philips' technological prowess.

Their success story is a powerful reminder of how technology, when harnessed with intention and strategy, can turn geographical divides into a source of strength and innovation.

> **Quick Thought:**
> *The true power of technology in remote work lies not in the sophistication of the tools but in their ability to connect people, foster collaboration, and streamline processes.*

Entrepreneurship in Action: Key Ingredients

- **Strategic Tool Selection:** Choose tools that align with your team's workflows, communication styles, and project management needs.
- **Comprehensive Training:** Ensure team members are proficient in using selected tools through comprehensive training and ongoing support.
- **Security and Privacy:** Prioritize tools that offer robust security features and compliance with data protection regulations to safeguard your team's work and client information.

Case Study: Trello's Integration Mastery for Remote Productivity

Overview: Trello, a web-based, Kanban-style list-making application, has become a staple for remote teams seeking to streamline project management and enhance productivity. Behind Trello's success is a philosophy that prioritizes simplicity, flexibility, and user-centric design, making it an indispensable tool for distributed teams worldwide.

Streamlining Collaboration: Trello's impact on remote team productivity is profound, offering a visual platform for tracking projects in real-time. Its intuitive interface allows teams to create boards for various projects, with lists and cards representing tasks and stages of completion. This visual approach to project management simplifies complex projects into manageable tasks, enabling remote teams to maintain focus and drive projects forward effectively.

Customization and Integration: A key factor in Trello's widespread adoption among remote teams is its highly customizable nature. Teams can tailor boards to fit their specific workflow needs, integrating a variety of Power-Ups (Trello's term for integrations and features) to enhance functionality. From calendar views and automation with Butler to direct integrations with applications like Slack and Google Drive, Trello's ecosystem supports a seamless workflow, bridging the gap between various tools used by remote teams.

Fostering Team Dynamics: Beyond its organizational capabilities, Trello plays a significant role in nurturing team dynamics and culture in a remote setting. The platform encourages transparency and accountability, as every team member has visibility into project progress and individual responsibilities. This openness fosters a culture of trust and collaboration, essential elements for remote team cohesion and productivity.

Adaptability and Continuous Improvement: Trello's evolution reflects a commitment to continuous improvement and adaptability. By regularly introducing new features and refining existing ones based on user feedback, Trello ensures that it remains at the forefront of project management solutions for remote teams. This iterative approach to development mirrors the agile methodology many remote teams employ, making Trello an ideal companion for teams striving for efficiency and innovation.

Trello's success in enhancing remote team productivity lies in its ability to combine simplicity with powerful customization and integration options. By providing a platform that adapts to the diverse needs of distributed teams, Trello exemplifies how technology can bring people together, fostering collaboration and efficiency regardless of physical location. As remote work continues to evolve, tools like Trello that prioritize user experience and adaptability will remain essential for teams looking to navigate the complexities of the digital workplace.

```
Pro Tip:
Regularly review and update your technology stack to
adapt to evolving team needs and advancements in
remote work technologies, ensuring your team always
operates at peak efficiency.
```

Exercise: Remote Technology Productivity Mastery

Technology Selection and Integration:

- **Digital Tool Selection Seminar:** Dive into the process of selecting digital tools that align with your team's specific needs, focusing on communication, collaboration, and project management. This seminar will guide you through evaluating tool functionality, user experience, and security to make informed decisions.

- **Integration Strategies Workshop:** Learn how to seamlessly integrate new technologies into your existing workflows. This workshop covers the principles of effective tool integration, including data migration, user adoption techniques, and the synchronization of multiple platforms to create a cohesive digital workspace.

Training and Adoption:

- **Comprehensive Training Program Design:** Develop a structured training program tailored to your team's technological proficiency and the specific tools adopted. This program should include hands-on sessions, Q&A forums, and continuous learning opportunities to ensure high adoption rates.
- **Adoption Tracking and Feedback Loops:** Implement methods to track adoption rates and gather feedback on new technologies. Participants will learn how to use surveys, analytics, and direct feedback to assess tool effectiveness and user satisfaction, enabling ongoing optimization.

Security and Compliance:

- **Security Best Practices Training:** Host a training session on the importance of security and privacy in remote work technologies. Cover essential topics such as data encryption, access controls, and compliance with industry regulations to safeguard your team and client information.

- **Privacy Policy and Compliance Workshop:** Guide your team through understanding and implementing privacy policies that comply with data protection laws. This workshop emphasizes creating a secure digital environment that protects sensitive information and builds trust with clients and team members.

Challenge for You:

Over the next three months, undertake a comprehensive review and optimization of your technology stack with a focus on enhancing remote team productivity. Begin with the selection and integration of a new digital tool, followed by the development and execution of a training program for your team. Monitor the adoption and effectiveness of the new technology, making adjustments based on team feedback and performance metrics. Additionally, conduct a security audit of your digital tools to ensure compliance with the latest data protection standards. Document the process, challenges encountered, and the outcomes of these initiatives to create a case study for your organization. This exercise aims to elevate your team's productivity through strategic technology use, ensuring a secure and efficient remote work environment.

Concluding Thoughts:

Harnessing technology for remote team productivity is not just about implementing the latest tools; it's about creating a culture of efficiency, security, and seamless collaboration. As we explore the potential of digital solutions to redefine the landscape of remote work, the insights from this chapter serve as a guide for leaders eager to embrace the digital revolution. By carefully selecting, integrating, and optimizing technological tools, you can bridge the gap between geographical distances and transform your remote team into a cohesive, productive unit. The journey towards technological empowerment is ongoing, requiring continuous learning, adaptability, and a commitment to excellence. Are you ready to take the next step in enhancing your remote team's productivity, ensuring that technology serves as a catalyst for connection, innovation, and success?

18

Developing Leadership Skills for the Digital Age

"The function of leadership is to produce more leaders, not more followers."
— Ralph Nader

The digital age has redefined the landscape of leadership, presenting a unique set of challenges and opportunities for those at the helm of remote and distributed teams. This chapter delves into the essential leadership skills and competencies required to navigate the complexities of the digital workplace. With the rise of remote work, leaders must adapt their strategies to foster connectivity, productivity, and engagement across geographically dispersed teams.

Emotional intelligence emerges as a cornerstone for effective digital-age leadership. It enables leaders to cultivate a deep understanding of their own emotions and those of their team members, facilitating communication, collaboration, and conflict resolution in a virtual setting. Leaders who master emotional intelligence can inspire trust, resilience, and a shared vision, even when face-to-face interactions are limited.

The transition to remote work demands a leadership approach that prioritizes empowerment, adaptability, and continuous learning. By developing skills in clear communication, building rapport, and promoting team autonomy, leaders can overcome the inherent challenges of remote work. This chapter guides entrepreneurs through the process of enhancing their leadership abilities to lead distributed teams with confidence and competence.

The digital workplace requires leaders to be more than just managers; they must be visionaries, coaches, and facilitators of change. This chapter explores the multifaceted role of digital-age leadership, from harnessing the power of technology to enhancing team dynamics in a virtual space.

Key leadership skills such as delegating effectively, fostering a culture of feedback, and navigating the intricacies of cross-cultural communication are dissected. Entrepreneurs will learn how to leverage these competencies to build cohesive, high-performing remote teams.

Opening Anecdote: HubSpot's Leadership Innovation

HubSpot, renowned for its inbound marketing and sales software, exemplifies innovative leadership in the digital age. Through its commitment to continuous learning and leadership development, HubSpot has cultivated a remote work culture that is both dynamic and inclusive. Their approach demonstrates how investing in leadership skills can empower teams, drive performance, and sustain growth in a digital environment.

> **Quick Thought:**
> *In the digital age, leadership is less about command and control and more about connection and empowerment.*

Entrepreneurship in Action: Key Ingredients

- **Emotional Intelligence:** Cultivate empathy and understanding to connect with team members on a deeper level.
- **Clear Communication:** Master the art of conveying ideas and expectations succinctly and effectively across digital platforms.
- **Team Empowerment:** Encourage autonomy and innovation by trusting team members to take ownership of their work.

Case Study: Anne-Laure Le Cunff's Mindful Leadership at Ness Labs

Overview: Anne-Laure Le Cunff, the founder of Ness Labs, has become a paragon for mindful leadership in the digital workspace. Ness Labs, a platform dedicated to fostering mindful productivity for knowledge workers, reflects Anne-Laure's commitment to combining productivity with well-being. Her approach to leadership, deeply rooted in principles of neuroscience and mindfulness, offers a unique perspective on guiding remote teams in the digital age.

Mindful Productivity: Under Anne-Laure's guidance,

Ness Labs champions the concept of mindful productivity, where the focus is on achieving goals without compromising mental health. This philosophy is integral to her leadership style, emphasizing the balance between productivity and well-being. Through workshops, articles, and community discussions, she actively promotes strategies that prevent burnout and encourage a healthy work-life balance among her remote team and the broader Ness Labs community.

Empowering Remote Teams: Anne-Laure's leadership is characterized by a strong emphasis on autonomy and empowerment. By leveraging digital tools and platforms, she has created an environment where team members are encouraged to take ownership of their projects, with the freedom to explore innovative solutions. Her approach underscores the importance of trust in remote team dynamics, where clear communication and support replace micromanagement.

Cultivating a Culture of Continuous Learning: At the heart of Ness Labs is a commitment to continuous learning and intellectual curiosity. Anne-Laure fosters this culture by curating resources, facilitating learning opportunities, and encouraging her team to dedicate time to personal and professional growth. This ethos of lifelong learning is not just about career development but also about nurturing a growth mindset that values creativity, experimentation, and resilience.

Technological Enablement: Recognizing the pivotal role of technology in enabling remote work, Anne-Laure has adeptly integrated various digital tools to streamline collaboration and communication within Ness Labs. From using asynchronous communication platforms to minimize disruptions to employing project management software that supports transparent workflows, her strategic use of technology enhances team productivity while supporting the company's mindful productivity ethos.

Anne-Laure Le Cunff's leadership at Ness Labs exemplifies how embracing innovation and continuous learning, coupled with a mindful approach to productivity, can cultivate a thriving remote work environment. Her success in building a community and business that resonates with knowledge workers globally serves as a testament to the effectiveness of mindful leadership in the digital age. By prioritizing well-being, autonomy, and lifelong learning, Anne-Laure not only leads by example but also empowers others to explore the full potential of their creative and intellectual capabilities in a supportive and enriching environment.

```
Pro Tip:
Integrate regular self-reflection and feedback
sessions into your leadership practice to
continually adapt and refine your approach to meet
the evolving needs of your remote team.
```

Exercise: Digital-Age Leadership Mastery

Enhancing Emotional Intelligence:

- **Emotional Awareness Exercise:** Reflect on recent leadership challenges and identify the emotions involved. Analyze how these emotions influenced your decision-making and interactions with the team. This exercise aims to improve your emotional awareness and its impact on leadership effectiveness.

- **Empathy Practice Session:** Conduct structured empathy-building activities, such as perspective-taking exercises or deep listening practices, to enhance your ability to understand and relate to your team members' experiences and viewpoints.

Communication in a Remote Context:

- **Digital Communication Simulation:** Engage in simulated digital communication scenarios to practice clarity, conciseness, and tone. Focus on overcoming common virtual communication barriers, such as misinterpretation and lack of non-verbal cues.
- **Feedback and Rapport Building Workshop:** Learn strategies for giving and receiving feedback in a remote setting. Practice building rapport through virtual team-building activities that foster open communication and trust.

Promoting Team Autonomy and Empowerment:

- **Delegation Dynamics Workshop:** Explore effective delegation techniques tailored for remote teams. This includes setting clear expectations, providing necessary resources, and establishing trust-based accountability measures.
- **Innovation Incubator Session:** Facilitate a session where team members can pitch ideas for improving workflows, processes, or projects. This promotes a culture of

innovation and empowers team members to take initiative and contribute to team goals.

Challenge for You:

Over the next three months, commit to enhancing a specific aspect of your leadership style that is crucial for the digital age. Choose one area of focus—emotional intelligence, communication, or team empowerment—and apply targeted strategies from this workshop. Track your progress through team feedback, self-assessment, and observable changes in team dynamics and performance. Document your journey, including the challenges faced, strategies implemented, and lessons learned, to serve as a leadership growth blueprint.

Concluding Thoughts:

Embracing leadership in the digital age is about more than adapting to new technologies; it's about cultivating a leadership style that thrives on connection, empathy, and empowerment across the digital divide. This chapter has laid the groundwork for developing leadership skills that resonate deeply with the needs of distributed teams, emphasizing the importance of emotional intelligence, clear communication, and fostering an environment of autonomy and growth. As we navigate this digital landscape, the ability to lead with vision and empathy becomes paramount. The journey ahead is filled with opportunities for growth, learning, and innovation. Are you ready to take on the mantle of leadership in the digital age, guiding your team with confidence, compassion, and unwavering commitment to collective success?

19

Adapting Leadership Approaches to Different Cultural Contexts

"Culture eats strategy for breakfast."
— Peter Drucker

Navigating the complex mosaic of global business, entrepreneurs today find themselves at the helm of teams as diverse as the world itself. The convergence of multiple cultures within a single team presents both a challenge and an opportunity for leadership. This chapter delves into the critical importance of adapting leadership approaches to resonate with different cultural contexts, a necessity in the ever-globalizing marketplace.

Understanding cultural nuances goes beyond mere acknowledgment; it involves a deep dive into the underlying dimensions that distinguish cultures. Through frameworks like Hofstede's Cultural Dimensions, leaders can gain insights into the societal values that influence team dynamics, decision-making, and communication preferences. Armed with this understanding, entrepreneurs can craft leadership strategies that are not just effective but also respectful and inclusive of cultural diversity.

At the core of navigating these multicultural waters is Cultural Intelligence (CQ) — the ability to relate and work effectively across cultures. Developing CQ is an ongoing journey of enhancing knowledge, mindfulness, and empathy. It empowers entrepreneurs to lead with a global mindset, fostering an environment where collaboration thrives across borders. This chapter guides leaders through building cross-cultural communication skills, establishing trust, and adapting leadership styles to thrive in the rich tapestry of global business.

The journey into effective cross-cultural leadership involves more than just a theoretical understanding of cultural dimensions. It requires leaders to actively engage in practices that build trust, respect, and a sense of belonging among diverse team members.

Practical strategies for enhancing cross-cultural communication and collaboration are explored, alongside insights into navigating the delicate balance of leadership and power distance in varying cultural contexts.

Opening Anecdote: Netflix's Cultural Agility

Netflix's leadership philosophy exemplifies the power of cultural adaptation. By empowering regional leaders to tailor content and strategies according to local cultural insights, Netflix has achieved unparalleled success on a global scale. This approach underscores the significance of understanding and respecting cultural differences in crafting a universally resonant brand.

> *Quick Thought:*
> *Leadership is the art of making genuine connections across cultural divides.*

Entrepreneurship in Action: Key Ingredients

- **Cultural Intelligence:** Elevate your leadership by continuously expanding your cultural knowledge and sensitivity.
- **Adaptive Communication:** Tailor your communication style to bridge cultural gaps and enhance team collaboration.
- **Inclusive Decision-Making:** Foster an environment where diverse perspectives are not only heard but are integral to decision-making.

Case Study: Toyota's Harmonizing Leadership Across Cultures

Toyota's global leadership philosophy, deeply rooted in the "Toyota Way," illustrates a sophisticated blend of steadfast principles and cultural adaptability. This unique approach enables Toyota to navigate the diverse cultural landscapes in which it operates, from North America and Europe to Asia and Africa. At the core of Toyota's success is its commitment to respect for people and continuous improvement, values that transcend geographical and cultural boundaries.

Principles Adapting to Cultures: Toyota's leadership does not impose a one-size-fits-all methodology; instead, it respects and integrates local cultural norms and practices. For instance, in Japan, the emphasis is on consensus-building and harmony, reflecting the cultural value of collectivism. Conversely, in the U.S., where individualism and assertiveness are more valued, Toyota adapts its leadership style to encourage more direct communication and personal accountability.

Cultural Intelligence in Practice: Toyota invests heavily in cultural training for its leaders, equipping them with the knowledge and skills to recognize and bridge cultural gaps. This includes understanding the nuances of communication styles, decision-making processes, and motivational factors across different cultures. Toyota's leaders are trained to be culturally intelligent, capable of adjusting their approach to leadership and communication to resonate with their diverse team members.

Empowering Local Leadership: A key component of Toyota's global strategy is empowering local leadership. By placing trust in local managers and allowing them to make decisions that align with regional cultural norms, Toyota ensures that its global operations are both cohesive and culturally sensitive. This localized approach to leadership fosters a sense of ownership and pride among team members, enhancing motivation and commitment.

Cross-Cultural Collaboration: Toyota promotes cross-cultural collaboration by creating mixed teams for international projects. These teams bring together diverse perspectives, fostering innovation and creative problem-solving. Toyota also facilitates cultural exchange programs, where employees have the opportunity to work in different countries, deepening their understanding of global operations and cultural nuances.

Toyota's approach to adapting leadership across different cultural contexts demonstrates the company's deep commitment to respecting and leveraging cultural diversity. By balancing the universal principles of the "Toyota Way" with local cultural insights, Toyota not only achieves global success but also cultivates an inclusive work environment that values and respects every team member's background. Other organizations looking to thrive in the global market can learn from Toyota's example, recognizing that cultural adaptability, respect, and continuous learning are key to effective leadership in diverse cultural settings.

```
Pro Tip:
Embrace cultural learning as a continuous journey.
Encourage your team to share their cultural
backgrounds and perspectives to enrich collective
understanding and cooperation.
```

Exercise: Cross-Cultural Leadership Workshop

Understanding Cultural Nuances:

- **Cultural Research Assignment:** Each team member selects a different culture present within the team or relevant to your business operations. Research and present key cultural dimensions and how they might impact team interactions, decision-making, and leadership approaches.
- **Cultural Dimensions Analysis:** Utilize Hofstede's Cultural Dimensions to analyze the primary cultures within

your team. Discuss how these dimensions influence work preferences, communication styles, and leadership perceptions, aiming to develop tailored leadership strategies.

Building Cultural Intelligence (CQ):

- **Self-Assessment on Cultural Intelligence:** Take a CQ self-assessment to identify personal strengths and areas for improvement. Set specific goals for enhancing your cultural understanding and adaptability.
- **Empathy Exercises:** Conduct exercises focused on developing empathy and understanding towards team members' cultural perspectives. This could include storytelling sessions where team members share personal experiences that highlight cultural values and norms.

Enhancing Cross-Cultural Communication:

- **Interactive Communication Workshops:** Engage in workshops designed to practice and refine cross-cultural communication skills. Focus on active listening, effective questioning, and adapting messaging to cultural contexts.
- **Feedback Loop Implementation:** Establish a feedback loop mechanism within the team to continuously improve cross-cultural communication. Encourage open and respectful feedback on communication styles and strategies.

Inclusive Decision-Making and Collaboration:

- **Inclusive Brainstorming Session:** Facilitate a brainstorming session that employs inclusive decision-making practices, ensuring diverse perspectives are considered and valued.

- **Collaboration Challenge:** Create a team project that requires input and collaboration from all cultural backgrounds represented in the team. Reflect on the collaborative process and outcomes, identifying lessons learned and best practices for future projects.

Challenge for You:

Select one aspect of your leadership approach that could be better adapted to the cultural contexts of your team. Over the next three months, focus on modifying this aspect, whether it's communication style, decision-making process, or feedback approach. Engage in continuous learning and reflection on cultural nuances, incorporating feedback from team members to gauge the effectiveness of your adaptations. Document the changes implemented, the challenges faced, and the impact on team cohesion and productivity.

Concluding Thoughts:

Navigating the complexities of leading across diverse cultural contexts requires a blend of empathy, adaptability, and an unwavering commitment to inclusivity. This chapter has illuminated the path toward understanding and embracing the rich tapestry of global cultures within your team, highlighting the transformative power of cultural intelligence in the realm of leadership. As we venture further into an increasingly connected world, the ability to adapt and thrive in a multitude of cultural landscapes becomes not just an advantage, but a necessity. The journey of cultural adaptation challenges us to grow, to broaden our perspectives, and to lead with a global mindset that values and harnesses diversity as a source of strength and innovation. Are you ready to embark on this journey, to deepen your cultural understanding, and to lead your team with a renewed sense of empathy and inclusivity, ensuring that every member feels valued, understood, and integral to the team's success?

20

Supporting Career Growth and Professional Development Remotely

"An investment in knowledge pays the best interest."
— Benjamin Franklin

I n the rapidly evolving digital landscape, the ability to support career growth and professional development remotely has become a cornerstone for successful leadership. Entrepreneurs face the unique challenge of nurturing their team's potential from afar, fostering an environment where continuous learning and career progression are not just encouraged but are integral to the team's ethos. This chapter explores the transformative strategies entrepreneurs can employ to cultivate a culture that champions professional growth, ensuring that remote teams remain engaged, motivated, and aligned with their career aspirations and the organization's goals.

Emphasizing lifelong learning and fostering a growth mind-set form the foundation of a development-focused culture. Entrepreneurs must navigate the digital space to provide accessible learning resources, encourage explorative learning experiences, and support risk-taking as a step toward innovation and personal growth. This environment not only propels team members toward their career objectives but also fortifies the organization's adaptability and resilience in the face of change.

The individualized approach to career development, through thoughtful planning, remote coaching, and virtual mentoring, personalizes the growth journey for each team member. Entrepreneurs can unlock the potential within their teams by setting clear, tailored goals, leveraging strengths, and providing the guidance needed to navigate professional landscapes. Through real-world examples and actionable strategies, this chapter outlines how to effectively champion and facilitate career growth and professional development within remote and distributed teams.

The journey of fostering professional development in remote settings is enriched with strategies for implementing individual development plans and utilizing remote coaching and mentoring to support employee growth.

Opening Anecdote: The Unilever Pathways Program

Unilever's commitment to supporting the career growth and professional development of its remote workforce shines brightly through its Pathways Program. This initiative provides employees with access to a diverse range of learning resources, mentorship opportunities, and career planning tools, all within a digital platform that transcends geographical limitations. Unilever's holistic approach not only aligns individual aspirations with the company's goals but also fosters a culture where continuous improvement and personal growth are celebrated as key drivers of organizational success.

> **Quick Thought:**
> *Empowerment through education is the pathway to innovation.*

Entrepreneurship in Action: Key Ingredients

- **Continuous Learning:** Cultivate an environment where learning is perpetual, and access to educational resources is unrestricted.
- **Growth Mindset:** Encourage a mindset where challenges are viewed as opportunities for growth and development.
- **Personalized Development Plans:** Collaborate with team members to create personalized development plans that reflect their career goals and aspirations.

Case Study: Buffer's Blueprint for Remote Development

Buffer, known for its transparent and employee-centric culture, provides a compelling model for supporting career growth and professional development remotely. Recognizing the challenges and opportunities of remote work, Buffer has implemented innovative strategies to ensure that team members feel supported, engaged, and motivated to pursue their career aspirations.

Annual Learning Stipend: Buffer distinguishes itself by

offering an annual learning stipend to each employee, empowering them to invest in their professional development through courses, conferences, or books. This initiative demonstrates Buffer's commitment to lifelong learning and its belief in the value of investing in employee growth.

Personal Development Plans: Buffer encourages each team member to create a Personal Development Plan (PDP), which is reviewed and updated regularly with their managers. These plans are tailored to individual career aspirations, skills they wish to develop, and goals they aim to achieve. The process ensures alignment between the employee's growth trajectory and Buffer's business objectives, fostering a sense of purpose and direction.

Remote Coaching and Mentoring: Understanding the importance of guidance and support, Buffer facilitates remote coaching and mentoring opportunities for its team members. Through structured mentorship programs, employees are matched with mentors who provide advice, share experiences, and offer insights to help them navigate their career paths and personal growth journeys.

Transparent Career Conversations: At Buffer, career conversations are a regular part of the employee experience. Managers and team members engage in open discussions about career aspirations, performance feedback, and potential growth opportunities within the company. These conversations are framed positively, focusing on strengths, achievements, and areas for development.

Cultivating a Growth Mindset: Buffer actively cultivates a growth mindset within its team by celebrating failures as learning opportunities and encouraging experimentation. This culture of continuous improvement and openness to change keeps the team resilient and adaptable, key qualities for thriving in a remote work environment.

Buffer's approach to supporting career growth and professional development remotely is characterized by its proactive investment in team members, personalized growth plans, and a culture that values learning and development as integral to both individual and organizational success. Other organizations looking to enhance their remote work culture can draw inspiration from Buffer's practices, recognizing that fostering professional growth is not only beneficial for employee satisfaction and retention but also for driving innovation and achieving business goals.

Pro Tip:
"Regularly revisit and refine development plans in partnership with team members to ensure alignment with evolving career goals and organizational needs."

Exercise: Remote Career Advancement Pathways

Foundations of a Growth-Focused Culture:

- **Lifelong Learning Plan:** Design a plan for each team member that incorporates continuous learning opportunities, integrating online courses, webinars, and self-paced learning into their regular workflow.
- **Growth Mindset Challenges:** Introduce monthly challenges that encourage team members to step outside their

comfort zones, documenting their experiences and lessons learned in a shared digital space.

Personalized Career Development:

- **Individual Development Plan (IDP) Creation:** Guide team members through the process of creating their IDPs, focusing on both short-term achievements and long-term career goals, emphasizing adaptability and alignment with remote work trends.
- **Virtual Mentoring Sessions:** Establish a structured mentoring program that matches team members with mentors within or outside the organization for regular virtual catch-ups, focusing on career guidance, skill development, and networking.

Leveraging Technology for Learning:

- **Digital Learning Library:** Compile a curated list of resources tailored to different career paths within your team. Include access to online platforms, industry-specific publications, and internal knowledge-sharing sessions.
- **Interactive Webinar Series:** Host a series of webinars led by industry experts, including Q&A sessions to foster interactive learning and exposure to new ideas and practices.

Encouraging Exploration and Risk-Taking:

- **Innovation Incubator:** Launch a virtual space for team members to pitch and develop innovative projects outside their regular responsibilities, offering support and resources to bring promising ideas to fruition.

- **Feedback and Reflection Roundtables:** Organize regular virtual roundtables where team members can share their experiences with explorative learning and risk-taking, discussing both successes and setbacks in a supportive environment.

Challenge for You:

Select two initiatives from the workshop to implement within your team, focusing on areas such as continuous learning, personalized development plans, or leveraging technology for learning. Over the next quarter, closely monitor the progress and engagement levels of your team members, gathering feedback to assess the effectiveness of these initiatives. Adjust and expand upon these strategies based on outcomes, aiming to embed a culture of continuous growth and development within your remote team.

Concluding Thoughts:

Cultivating a culture where career growth and professional development flourish remotely requires dedication, foresight, and a commitment to each team member's individual journey. As we navigate through the strategies and insights provided in this chapter, the path to fostering a learning environment that transcends physical boundaries becomes clear. By embracing the principles of continuous learning, personalized development, and the strategic use of technology, leaders have the opportunity to not only enhance the skills and satisfaction of their team members but also to drive the innovation and agility of their organizations in the digital age. The journey towards creating a remote work culture that prioritizes development and growth is both challenging and rewarding, offering a new horizon of possibilities for team engagement and organizational success. Are you prepared to embark on this transformative path, ensuring that your team not only achieves their professional goals but also contributes to the overarching vision and success of your organization?

21

Nurturing Mentorship and Coaching in a Distributed Environment

"The delicate balance of mentoring someone is not creating them in your own image, but giving them the opportunity to create themselves."
— Steven Spielberg

I n the dynamic world of remote work, mentorship and coaching emerge as pivotal elements in the tapestry of professional development. Entrepreneurs leading distributed teams face the unique challenge of fostering these vital relationships without the traditional cues and contexts provided by physical proximity. This chapter delves into the nuanced strategies required to cultivate effective mentorship and coaching in a digital realm, emphasizing the importance of these relationships in facilitating growth, enhancing skills, and reinforcing the cohesion and morale of remote teams.

Understanding the roles mentors and coaches play in a distributed context sets the foundation for developing a nurturing environment conducive to learning and development.

Mentors, with their wealth of experience and wisdom, act as guides and confidants, offering advice and sharing insights that illuminate the path forward. Coaches, through targeted questions and structured support, empower individuals to explore their potential, set actionable goals, and navigate the challenges of their professional journeys with confidence.

Building a culture that embraces mentorship and coaching involves intentional design and thoughtful implementation. Entrepreneurs must leverage technology to bridge the gap created by distance, establishing platforms and practices that facilitate meaningful connections, enable knowledge sharing, and support the personal and professional growth of every team member. Through practical examples and actionable advice, this chapter provides a roadmap for creating impactful mentorship and coaching experiences that enrich the remote work environment and drive the collective success of distributed teams.

The chapter further explores the implementation of coaching frameworks and the use of virtual mentoring platforms, detailing how these elements contribute to the development of a supportive, growth-oriented remote work culture.

Opening Anecdote: Google's "Career Guru" Program

Google's innovative "Career Guru" program exemplifies the power of virtual mentorship in a global company. By pairing employees with seasoned Googlers, the initiative harnesses the potential of mentorship to guide, inspire, and open doors to new opportunities. This approach, supported by virtual platforms and rich resources, underscores the value of nurturing connections that transcend geographical boundaries, fostering a culture of continuous growth and development.

> ***Quick Thought:***
> *Investing in people through mentorship and coaching is investing in the future of your organization.*

Entrepreneurship in Action: Key Ingredients

- **Intentional Pairing:** Match mentors and mentees based on shared interests, goals, and expertise to foster meaningful relationships.
- **Structured Support:** Implement coaching frameworks that guide individuals in goal setting, action planning, and reflecting on progress.
- **Technological Enablement:** Leverage virtual platforms to facilitate mentorship and coaching, ensuring accessibility and engagement across distances.

Case Study: Microsoft's Virtual Leadership Development

Microsoft's "Manager as Coach" initiative showcases a forward-thinking approach to nurturing mentorship and coaching within a distributed environment. Recognizing the critical role of leadership development in fostering a culture of growth and empowerment, Microsoft has crafted a program that equips managers with the skills necessary to guide their teams through the complexities of remote work.

Emphasizing Coaching Skills in Leadership: At the heart

of Microsoft's program is the belief that effective leadership in a remote setting requires a coaching mindset. Managers are trained to adopt coaching techniques that emphasize listening, asking powerful questions, and facilitating the professional growth of their team members. This focus on developing coaching skills among leaders ensures that mentorship is woven into the fabric of daily interactions, creating a continuous learning environment.

Leveraging Technology for Remote Development: Microsoft utilizes its suite of collaboration tools to support these mentoring and coaching efforts. Platforms like Microsoft Teams become spaces where managers and their teams engage in regular one-on-one check-ins, set development goals, and track progress. The integration of these tools into the mentoring process ensures that communication remains consistent and impactful, regardless of the physical distances.

Structured Mentorship Programs: Microsoft also implements structured mentorship programs that pair employees with leaders across the organization. These programs are supported by digital platforms that facilitate scheduling, goal setting, and resource sharing, making mentorship accessible to all employees, regardless of their location. By providing clear frameworks and expectations for these relationships, Microsoft fosters meaningful connections that support career development and cross-functional learning.

Cultural Sensitivity and Global Perspectives: Understanding the global nature of its workforce, Microsoft places a strong emphasis on cultural sensitivity within its mentorship and coaching initiatives. Training programs for managers include modules on cultural awareness and communication styles, preparing them to effectively lead and mentor team members from diverse backgrounds. This commitment to cultural sensitivity ensures that mentorship and coaching are inclusive and respectful of the varied perspectives within the team.

Outcome and Impact: The results of Microsoft's "Manager as Coach" program and its broader mentorship initiatives speak volumes. Employees report a greater sense of engagement, a clearer path to career progression, and a stronger connection to the organization's mission. Furthermore, managers equipped with coaching skills are better able to navigate the challenges of remote leadership, fostering team cohesion and driving performance.

Microsoft's approach to mentorship and coaching in a distributed environment demonstrates that with thoughtful planning, commitment to leadership development, and the strategic use of technology, it is possible to cultivate a culture of growth and empowerment that spans the globe. This case study serves as a beacon for other organizations striving to support the professional development of their remote teams, proving that distance is no barrier to impactful mentorship and effective leadership.

```
Pro Tip:
"Create a mentoring and coaching feedback loop,
where participants can share their experiences and
learnings, continually refining the process for
greater impact."
```

Exercise: Virtual Mentorship and Coaching Catalyst

Foundations of Effective Virtual Mentorship:

- **Mentor-Mentee Compatibility Quiz:** Develop a quiz to assess the interests, goals, and career aspirations of participants, facilitating more meaningful and productive mentor-mentee pairings.
- **Mentorship Roadmap Creation:** Guide mentors and mentees in co-creating a roadmap for their relationship, including setting specific objectives, milestones, and regular check-in points to assess progress and adapt goals as needed.

Coaching for Remote Team Success:

- **Coaching Skills Bootcamp:** Conduct an interactive virtual bootcamp for aspiring coaches, covering key skills such as goal-setting methodologies, active listening techniques, and the art of providing constructive feedback.
- **Action Planning Workshop:** Work with team members to develop personalized action plans, outlining steps to achieve professional development goals and how coaching can support their journey.

Leveraging Technology for Connection:

- **Virtual Mentorship Platform Demo:** Showcase different virtual platforms that can facilitate mentorship and coaching interactions, discussing features that enable effective communication, schedule management, and resource sharing.

- **Digital Resource Library Assembly:** Compile a comprehensive digital library of resources for both mentors and mentees, including articles, videos, and templates that support the mentorship process.

Building a Culture of Continuous Learning:

- **Feedback and Reflection Circles:** Initiate monthly virtual gatherings for sharing experiences, challenges, and successes within the mentorship and coaching programs, fostering a community of learning and support.
- **Growth Showcase Event:** Organize a quarterly virtual event where mentors and mentees present on their progress, learnings, and how the mentorship has impacted their professional development.

Challenge for You:

Select two initiatives from the workshop to introduce to your team, focusing on areas such as mentor-mentee matching, coaching skills development, or leveraging technology for better connection. Over the next quarter, closely monitor the participation and feedback, adjusting the program based on insights gained to enhance the effectiveness of your mentorship and coaching efforts in the distributed environment.

Concluding Thoughts:

Fostering mentorship and coaching in a distributed environment demands creativity, commitment, and a deep understanding of the digital landscape's unique challenges and opportunities. As we navigate through the strategies outlined in this chapter, it becomes evident that the power of mentorship and coaching extends far beyond traditional office boundaries, thriving in the virtual world where connections are not limited by geography. By intentionally pairing mentors and mentees, offering structured support, and leveraging technology to bridge distances, leaders can cultivate a culture of growth, development, and mutual support that transcends physical limitations. This journey of fostering mentorship and coaching in remote settings is not merely about replicating in-person experiences digitally but about reimagining these relationships in a way that leverages the strengths of virtual platforms to inspire, guide, and empower individuals across the globe. Are you ready to harness the potential of virtual mentorship and coaching to create a more connected, empowered, and resilient remote team?

22

Leading Distributed Teams Through Change and Transformation

"To improve is to change; to be perfect is to change often."
— Winston Churchill

Navigating the turbulent waters of change in the digital landscape demands from entrepreneurs not just a vision but a profound understanding of the unique dynamics at play within distributed teams. The rapid pace of technological advancements, coupled with the global nature of remote work, introduces complexities that require an agile and informed leadership approach. This chapter embarks on a journey to explore the intricacies of steering distributed teams through the ebbs and flows of change and transformation, emphasizing the critical role of adaptability, resilience, and strategic communication.

At the heart of successfully managing change lies the ability to foster resilience and adaptability within a team that is geographically dispersed. Entrepreneurs must nurture these qualities, providing the scaffolding for remote team members to not only withstand the shocks of change but to thrive amidst them. This resilience becomes a beacon of strength, guiding teams through uncertainty and enabling them to emerge more cohesive and robust on the other side of transformation.

Developing a strategic plan for communication and collaboration is pivotal in the process of managing change. Entrepreneurs are tasked with crafting a blueprint that leverages technology to bridge distances, ensuring transparent, timely, and effective communication. This plan should not only convey the what and the why behind the change but also actively engage team members in dialogue, fostering a sense of inclusion and collective endeavor. By empowering remote team members as agents of change, entrepreneurs can unlock the full potential of their distributed teams, driving successful transformation across the digital expanse.

Further sections delve into the importance of inclusive decision-making and empowering team members as change agents, along with leveraging technological tools to enhance collaboration and maintain engagement during times of change.

Opening Anecdote: The IBM Blueprint for Transformation

IBM's leadership through decades of industry change showcases a blueprint for mastering transformation in the remote work era. By embracing open communication, fostering adaptability, and empowering its global team, IBM has navigated shifts in technology and market demand with resilience and foresight. Their approach to leading through change, characterized by transparency, innovation, and a steadfast commitment to employee development, serves as a guiding light for companies navigating their paths through the digital transformation landscape.

> **Quick Thought:**
> *Change presents a doorway to progress. Leading with empathy and clarity can transform challenges into opportunities for growth.*

Entrepreneurship in Action: Key Ingredients

- **Transparent Communication:** Ensure clear, open dialogue about changes, providing the rationale and expected outcomes.
- **Technological Integration:** Use collaboration tools and platforms to maintain connectivity and engagement.
- **Empowerment:** Involve team members in the change process, recognizing their contributions as essential to success.

Case Study: Duolingo's Approach to Distributed Team Management

Background: Duolingo, a language learning platform, has revolutionized educational technology with its user-friendly app that makes learning new languages accessible to millions worldwide. Behind its success is a distributed team that spans several continents, driven by a leadership style that emphasizes adaptability, inclusivity, and continuous innovation.

Leadership at the Core: Luis von Ahn, co-founder and

CEO of Duolingo, has been instrumental in steering the company through periods of rapid growth and significant change. His approach combines visionary product development with a keen focus on creating a supportive environment for a globally distributed team. Von Ahn's leadership is characterized by open communication, a commitment to employee well-being, and fostering a culture of continuous learning.

Embracing Change: As Duolingo entered new markets and continuously updated its offerings to enhance user experience, the company faced the challenge of ensuring that its remote team remained cohesive and aligned with its goals. Von Ahn led by example, promoting a culture where change is seen as an opportunity for growth. He implemented regular, transparent updates and virtual town halls to discuss strategic shifts, ensuring that every team member, regardless of location, felt connected to the company's mission.

Innovative Solutions for Remote Collaboration: Duolingo's leadership invested in cutting-edge collaboration tools and created bespoke processes to facilitate effective teamwork across different time zones. They introduced asynchronous communication practices to accommodate the global nature of their team, minimizing the strain of coordinating across wide geographical divides. This approach ensured that creativity and productivity thrived, even in a fully remote setting.

Outcome: Under Von Ahn's leadership, Duolingo has not only expanded its user base but also maintained a strong company culture that values diversity, inclusivity, and innovation. The company's ability to adapt to change and leverage the strengths of its distributed team has been key to its success in making language learning fun, effective, and accessible to all.

Legacy of Leadership: Duolingo's journey highlights the effectiveness of adaptive leadership in managing distributed teams. Von Ahn's strategies in embracing technology for collaboration, prioritizing open communication, and encouraging a culture of innovation serve as a blueprint for other companies navigating the complexities of the digital age.

This case study exemplifies how a commitment to leadership development, employee empowerment, and embracing change can transform challenges into opportunities for innovation and global success.

```
Pro Tip:
Anticipate the emotional journey of change.
Addressing concerns and fostering dialogue can
smooth the path to transformation.
```

Exercise: Navigating Change in Distributed Teams

Foundations of Adaptive Leadership:

- **Adaptability Assessment:** Begin with an assessment for leaders and team members to identify current adaptability levels and areas for growth. Utilize insights to tailor leadership strategies to individual and team needs.
- **Resilience Building Exercises:** Conduct workshops focusing on building resilience through scenario-based learning, teaching team members to develop flexible responses to unexpected changes.

Strategic Communication Framework:

- **Change Communication Plan Development:** Guide leaders through the creation of detailed communication plans for upcoming changes, including timelines, channels, key messages, and feedback loops.
- **Empathy Mapping Session:** Utilize empathy maps to understand diverse team member perspectives on change, refining communication strategies to address various needs and concerns.

Inclusive Decision-Making Process:

- **Collaborative Decision-Making Workshop:** Facilitate a session on inclusive decision-making, highlighting techniques for engaging remote team members in the change process.
- **Change Agent Identification:** Develop criteria for identifying and empowering change agents within the team, followed by an action plan to activate their roles effectively.

Technological Tools for Engaging Change Management:

- **Digital Tools Showcase:** Present and demo collaboration and project management tools that facilitate seamless communication and project tracking during periods of change.
- **Virtual Brainstorming Lab:** Host a virtual brainstorming session using collaborative online tools to generate innovative solutions for potential challenges during the transformation process.

Challenge for You:

Select one upcoming change initiative and apply the communication and engagement strategies developed in this workshop. Over the following three months, closely monitor the initiative's implementation, focusing on team engagement, feedback incorporation, and the overall effectiveness of the change process. Adjust strategies based on real-time insights and team feedback to refine your approach to leading through change.

Concluding Thoughts:

Steering distributed teams through the landscapes of change and transformation requires not just vision but an intricate understanding of the dynamics that underpin remote collaboration. As we unravel the strategies for managing change, it becomes clear that adaptability, resilience, and strategic communication are not mere buzzwords but essential pillars that support the journey through change. The ability to foster these qualities within a team, coupled with leveraging technology for effective communication, empowers leaders to turn the challenges of change into opportunities for growth and innovation. By involving team members as active participants in the change process and fostering a culture of openness and empowerment, leaders can ensure that their teams not only navigate change successfully but emerge stronger, more united, and better equipped for the future.

Are you prepared to lead your team through the transformative journey of change, harnessing the power of adaptability, resilience, and collective endeavor to thrive in the digital age?

23

Building Resilience and Managing Remote Team Dynamics

"Coming together is a beginning. Keeping together is progress.

Working together is success."
— Henry Ford

I n the sprawling digital workspace where boundaries blur and the traditional office is redefined, the resilience of a team becomes its backbone, enabling it to thrive amidst volatility and uncertainty. For entrepreneurs steering these distributed teams, fostering resilience and effectively managing remote dynamics are paramount. This chapter delves into the essence of building a team not just to withstand the inevitable challenges of remote work but to emerge stronger, more cohesive, and agile.

Trust and psychological safety lay the groundwork for resilience in a remote context, serving as the pillars upon which open communication, risk-taking, and innovation stand. Entrepreneurs play a pivotal role in cultivating these qualities, ensuring that remote team members feel valued, understood, and secure. It's about creating an environment where failures are seen as stepping stones to success, where every voice is heard, and where the collective goal transcends individual achievements.

Promoting a positive team culture amidst a distributed setup requires deliberate actions and consistent communication of shared values. It's about celebrating milestones, no matter the physical distance, and recognizing the small wins that fuel the journey towards larger goals. By setting clear expectations, facilitating seamless collaboration, and embracing the unique dynamics of remote work, entrepreneurs can lead their teams through the complexities of change, fostering resilience and driving transformation across digital landscapes.

Further exploration into clear goal setting, effective communication strategies, and leveraging technology for collaboration illuminates the path for entrepreneurs to manage remote team dynamics successfully.

Opening Anecdote: The Ernst & Young (EY) Resilience Framework

Ernst & Young (EY), a global leader in assurance, tax, and consulting services, exemplifies building resilience and managing remote team dynamics through its comprehensive Resilience Framework. By intertwining emotional intelligence training with strategic communication practices, EY ensures that its remote workforce is equipped to handle the pressures and challenges of the digital age. Their structured approach to fostering a supportive, adaptive, and cohesive team environment, even in the face of rapid change and uncertainty, illustrates the profound impact of resilience on team performance and well-being.

> **Quick Thought:**
> *Building a resilient team is like weaving a strong fabric—each thread, when woven with care and consideration, contributes to a tapestry that can withstand the test of time and change.*

Entrepreneurship in Action: Key Ingredients

- **Transparent Communication:** Cultivate an environment where open, honest dialogue is the norm.
- **Emphasis on Well-being:** Prioritize the physical and mental health of team members as a cornerstone of resilience.
- **Celebration of Achievements:** Recognize and celebrate the milestones achieved, fostering a sense of collective pride and motivation.

Case Study: Zapier's Culture of Resilience and Adaptability

Zapier, a leader in automation for web applications, exemplifies the essence of building resilience and managing remote team dynamics effectively. With a workforce that spans across various time zones and cultures, Zapier has mastered the art of fostering a resilient team culture that is both flexible and cohesive.

Emphasizing Trust and Psychological Safety: At the core

of Zapier's approach is a deep emphasis on trust and psychological safety. The company has cultivated an environment where open communication and transparency are paramount. Regular "ask me anything" (AMA) sessions with leadership and open forums for feedback ensure that team members feel valued and heard. This openness encourages risk-taking and innovation, essential components of a resilient team.

Leveraging Technology for Effective Collaboration: Understanding the challenges of remote work, Zapier leverages a suite of digital tools to enhance collaboration and maintain a strong team connection. Tools like Slack for communication, Trello for project management, and Zoom for video conferencing are integrated seamlessly into daily operations, ensuring that team members can collaborate efficiently despite geographical distances.

Promoting Well-being and Work-Life Balance: Zapier places a high priority on the well-being and work-life balance of its employees. Initiatives like mandatory vacation time and "no meeting" days help prevent burnout and promote a healthy work-life balance. By recognizing the human aspect of work, Zapier ensures that its team remains motivated and engaged, critical factors for building resilience.

Celebrating Achievements and Fostering Development: Understanding the importance of recognition in building team morale, Zapier has implemented innovative programs to celebrate both individual and team achievements. The use of digital kudos, public shout-outs, and achievement-based rewards reinforces a culture of appreciation and motivates continuous improvement.

Moreover, Zapier invests in the professional development of its team members through online courses, workshops, and conferences. This commitment to growth not only enhances individual skill sets but also contributes to the team's overall resilience and adaptability.

Outcome and Impact: Zapier's strategic focus on building a resilient remote team has resulted in impressive outcomes. The company enjoys high levels of employee satisfaction, low turnover rates, and sustained productivity, all of which contribute to its continuous growth and success in the competitive tech industry.

Zapier's approach to nurturing mentorship and coaching in a distributed environment demonstrates that with the right strategies, commitment to employee well-being, and effective use of technology, it is possible to cultivate a culture of resilience and adaptability. This case study serves as an inspiration for other organizations navigating the complexities of remote work, proving that distance is no barrier to creating a strong, cohesive, and resilient team.

```
Pro Tip:
Embed resilience into the DNA of your remote team by
leading with empathy, encouraging continuous
learning, and embracing change as an opportunity for
growth.
```

Exercise: Cultivating Team Resilience in Remote Environments

Trust Building and Psychological Safety:

- **Trust-Building Activities:** Initiate virtual activities that enhance trust within the team, such as virtual team-building exercises or shared storytelling sessions, focusing on personal growth and professional challenges.
- **Psychological Safety Roundtable:** Facilitate discussions on creating a psychologically safe work environment where team members feel comfortable expressing themselves without fear of negative consequences.

Effective Communication and Collaboration:

- **Communication Channels Review:** Assess current communication channels and protocols to ensure they support open and transparent dialogue. Identify any gaps and plan improvements.
- **Collaboration Efficiency Workshop:** Conduct a workshop aimed at optimizing remote collaboration, exploring best practices and tools that enhance team interaction and productivity.

Well-being and Work-Life Balance:

- **Well-being Workshops:** Organize sessions focused on mental health and well-being, including stress management techniques and the importance of work-life balance.
- **Digital Detox Challenges:** Encourage team members to

participate in digital detox challenges, emphasizing the importance of unplugging to maintain mental health and productivity.

Recognition and Celebration of Achievements:

- **Achievement Recognition Program:** Develop a program for recognizing individual and team achievements, including virtual awards or acknowledgments in team meetings.
- **Milestone Celebrations:** Plan virtual events to celebrate project milestones and team achievements, reinforcing a sense of accomplishment and collective success.

Challenge for You:

Over the next six months, implement a resilience-building program that incorporates elements of trust, psychological safety, effective communication, and well-being. Track the program's impact on team dynamics, morale, and overall productivity, adjusting the approach based on feedback and observed outcomes.

Concluding Thoughts:

As we navigate the complexities of managing remote teams in an ever-evolving digital landscape, the importance of resilience and adaptability cannot be overstated. Building a team that not only survives but thrives through the challenges of remote work demands a leadership approach rooted in trust, psychological safety, and a commitment to open communication. By fostering an environment that values well-being, celebrates achievements, and encourages a culture of continuous learning and growth, entrepreneurs can empower their teams to navigate the uncertainties of the digital age with confidence and agility.

The journey towards fostering a resilient team is marked by deliberate actions and strategic communication, emphasizing the importance of each team member's contribution to the collective goal. As we look towards the future, the role of technology in facilitating collaboration and maintaining connectivity becomes increasingly critical, serving as a bridge that connects dispersed team members across the digital divide.

Are you prepared to embrace the challenges and opportunities of leading a distributed team, implementing strategies that bolster resilience, foster adaptability, and drive transformation? The path to building a strong, cohesive team in the digital age is paved with intention, empathy, and a steadfast commitment to supporting each team member's journey towards personal and professional growth.

24

Embracing Innovation and Continuous Learning in the Digital World

"Without tradition, art is a flock of sheep without a shepherd.
Without innovation, it is a corpse."
— Winston Churchill

I n the relentless march of technological progress, innovation and continuous learning emerge not just as strategies, but as imperatives for survival and success. For entrepreneurs navigating the vast and ever-changing digital landscape, fostering an environment that champions these principles is key to staying ahead. This chapter dives deep into the essence of innovation and the cultivation of a culture of continuous learning, revealing how they can propel remote teams to unprecedented heights of creativity and efficiency.

At the heart of innovation lies the willingness to explore, experiment, and embrace the unknown. Entrepreneurs must instill these values in their teams, encouraging a mindset that sees beyond the horizon of current knowledge and capabilities. Through the principles of innovation—creativity, experimentation, collaboration, and calculated risk-taking— entrepreneurs can unlock the potential of their distributed teams, driving them to discover solutions and opportunities that redefine their markets.

Cultivating a growth mindset and a culture of continuous learning within remote teams is more than an investment in skills; it's an investment in the future. By promoting a philosophy where challenges are seen as opportunities for growth, setbacks as lessons, and curiosity as a virtue, entrepreneurs can inspire their teams to continually evolve. Leveraging technology to access a world of learning resources and collaborative opportunities, they can ensure that their teams are not just prepared for the future but are actively shaping it.

Further exploration into the benefits of innovation and continuous learning, along with the implementation of structured programs like Atlassian's "ShipIt Days," provides a blueprint for entrepreneurs to invigorate their teams with the spirit of innovation.

Opening Anecdote: Google's 20% Time Policy

Google's innovative "20% Time" policy stands as a testament to the power of giving employees the freedom to explore their passions. This initiative, which led to the creation of products like Gmail and Google Maps, showcases how allocated time for innovation can result in groundbreaking developments. Entrepreneurs can draw inspiration from this example, recognizing that providing space for creativity and exploration within remote teams can spark innovations that propel the company forward.

> **Quick Thought:**
> *Innovation is the calling card of the future.*

Entrepreneurship in Action: Key Ingredients

- **Structured Innovation Time:** Like Google, allocate specific times for team members to work on projects outside their regular responsibilities.
- **Interactive Learning Sessions:** Host virtual workshops and webinars to facilitate continuous learning and skill development within the team.

Case Study: Atlassian's Commitment to Innovation and Learning

Atlassian, renowned for its collaboration and productivity software, has become a beacon for companies aiming to weave innovation and continuous learning into the fabric of their remote work culture. Their "ShipIt Days," a 24-hour hackathon where employees are encouraged to work on anything that sparks their interest, stands as a testament to Atlassian's dedication to fostering an environment where exploration and creativity are paramount.

Structured Innovation Programs: Atlassian's approach to innovation is characterized by structured yet flexible programs that allow employees to experiment and pursue passion projects. These initiatives not only serve as a powerful catalyst for groundbreaking ideas and improvements but also significantly enhance team engagement and morale. By dedicating time and resources to innovation, Atlassian demonstrates a profound understanding that the future of the company lies in the hands of its empowered and creatively fulfilled team members.

Embracing Continuous Learning: Beyond innovation sprints, Atlassian places a strong emphasis on continuous learning and development. Through their extensive use of digital learning platforms and the provision of resources for professional growth, Atlassian ensures that its team members have access to the latest knowledge and skills necessary to thrive in the digital age. This commitment to lifelong learning is integral to maintaining a competitive edge and adapting to the rapidly changing technological landscape.

Cultivating a Growth Mindset

Atlassian's culture is deeply rooted in the principles of a growth mindset. Employees are encouraged to view challenges as opportunities, embrace feedback, and learn from failures. This philosophy is critical in building resilience and adaptability, qualities that are essential for both personal and professional development in a remote work setting.

Leveraging Technology for Collaboration and Learning: The effective use of technology underpins Atlassian's strategies for innovation and learning. Platforms like Trello for project management and Confluence for knowledge sharing facilitate seamless collaboration across global teams, ensuring that ideas and insights are freely exchanged and that projects move forward efficiently.

Outcome and Impact: The impact of Atlassian's dedication to innovation and continuous learning is evident in its product development, employee satisfaction, and market success. By fostering an environment where team members are encouraged to explore, learn, and grow, Atlassian has not only enhanced its product offerings but also cultivated a workforce that is engaged, motivated, and aligned with the company's vision.

Atlassian's approach to nurturing innovation and lifelong learning among its remote workforce exemplifies the transformative power of embracing creativity and development in the digital workspace. Their success serves as a blueprint for other organizations striving to empower their teams, drive innovation, and foster a culture of continuous growth and adaptation. This case study underscores the importance of structured innovation programs, continuous learning opportunities, and a supportive culture in achieving organizational success and employee fulfillment in the modern work environment.

```
Pro Tip:
Embrace failure as a stepping stone to innovation.
The most successful innovations often come from
learning what doesn't work.
```

Exercise: Cultivating Innovation and Lifelong Learning

Innovation Incubator:

- **Idea Pitch Platform:** Establish a virtual forum where team members can pitch innovative ideas or projects,

fostering a culture where creativity is encouraged and valued.
- **Innovation Sprint Week:** Dedicate a week where team members work on selected ideas, applying the principles of fast prototyping and collaborative experimentation.

Continuous Learning Culture:

- **Digital Learning Library:** Create a centralized repository of online courses, webinars, and resources to promote skill development and continuous learning among team members.
- **Learning Circles:** Organize small, virtual discussion groups focused on specific areas of interest or new technologies, encouraging knowledge sharing and collaborative learning.

Experimentation and Risk-Taking:

- **Failure Forums:** Host regular sessions where team members can share experiences of failure in a supportive environment, highlighting lessons learned and fostering a positive attitude towards risk-taking.
- **Experimentation Grants:** Provide small budgets for team members to explore new tools, technologies, or methodologies, encouraging exploration and experimentation.

Growth Mindset Development:

- **Mindset Workshops:** Facilitate workshops on developing a growth mindset, emphasizing the value of challenges, persistence, and adaptability in personal and professional growth.

- **Personal Growth Plans:** Work with team members to develop personalized growth plans that include both professional objectives and personal development goals.

Challenge for You: Initiate a "Month of Learning" challenge within your team, encouraging members to dedicate time to learning a new skill or exploring a new area of interest. Host weekly check-ins to share insights and progress, culminating in a showcase of what was learned or created.

Concluding Thoughts:

Leading through innovation and embracing continuous learning are essential in navigating the digital age's complexities. This chapter has illuminated the path for fostering an environment where creativity and efficiency propel remote teams to new heights. The challenge now lies in implementing these strategies, from providing structured innovation time like Google's "20% Time" to embracing failure as a stepping stone to success. The future of your team and organization hinges on the ability to continuously adapt and grow in a landscape that is ever-evolving. Are you ready to lead your team on this journey of endless innovation and learning, ensuring that they are not only prepared for the future but are also actively shaping it?

25

Looking Ahead: Future Trends in Leading and Managing Distributed Teams

As technology evolves and remote work becomes more prevalent, the future of leading and managing distributed teams holds exciting possibilities. In this chapter, we will explore emerging trends and insights that can shape the way entrepreneurs navigate the challenges and opportunities of remote team management. By staying informed and adaptable, leaders can position themselves for success in the ever-changing landscape of distributed work.

Leveraging Artificial Intelligence and Automation
AI-Driven Talent Acquisition and Onboarding

Artificial intelligence (AI) can revolutionize the way entrepreneurs find and onboard remote team members. AI-powered algorithms can help identify candidates with the right skills and cultural fit, streamlining the recruitment process. Additionally, chatbots and virtual assistants can enhance the onboarding experience by providing automated guidance and support.

Automation for Streamlined Workflows

Automation technologies can significantly impact remote team productivity. Entrepreneurs can leverage robotic process automation (RPA) and workflow management tools to automate repetitive tasks, allowing team members to focus on higher-value work. This can lead to increased efficiency and improved outcomes.

Enhancing Collaboration through Virtual Reality (VR) and Augmented Reality (AR)

Immersive Virtual Meetings and Team Collaboration

Virtual reality (VR) and augmented reality (AR) can potentially transform remote team collaboration. With VR headsets and AR applications, team members can participate in virtual meetings, brainstorming sessions, and training programs as if physically present. This technology can foster a stronger sense of connection and improve collaboration among distributed teams.

Virtual Workspaces for Remote Team Productivity

Virtual workspaces enable remote team members to work together in a shared digital environment. These spaces can simulate physical offices, providing opportunities for spontaneous interactions, virtual whiteboarding, and seamless collaboration. Entrepreneurs can explore virtual workspace platforms like Spatial and VirBELA to enhance team productivity and engagement.

Data-Driven Performance Management and Analytics
Predictive Analytics for Team Performance

Advancements in data analytics can offer valuable insights into remote team performance. By analyzing data on individual and team productivity, entrepreneurs can identify patterns, predict future performance, and make data-driven decisions to optimize team outcomes.

Sentiment Analysis and Employee Well-being

Monitoring employee well-being and sentiment is crucial for remote team management. Text and sentiment analysis tools can help entrepreneurs gauge the emotional state of team members, identify potential issues, and take proactive steps to support their well-being.

Continued Emphasis on Cybersecurity and Data Privacy
Strengthening Remote Security Measures

With the increase in remote work, cybersecurity and data privacy become even more critical. Entrepreneurs must stay vigilant and invest in robust security measures to protect sensitive data and ensure secure communication and collaboration among remote team members.

Compliance with Changing Data Protection Regulations

As data protection regulations evolve, entrepreneurs must stay informed and ensure compliance with relevant laws such as the General Data Protection Regulation (GDPR) and the California Consumer Privacy Act (CCPA). This involves implementing appropriate data protection practices and keeping remote team members educated about their responsibilities regarding data privacy.

The future of leading and managing distributed teams holds immense potential. By embracing emerging technologies, leveraging data-driven insights, and prioritizing cybersecurity, entrepreneurs can stay ahead of the curve and drive success in remote team management. However, it is crucial to remain adaptable and open to evolving trends as the remote work landscape continues to evolve.

Epilogue: Navigating the Digital Frontier

As we draw the curtains on this digital odyssey, we stand at the threshold of a future pulsating with infinite possibilities. Through the chapters of "Digital Triumph," we've journeyed together across the vast expanse of the digital realm, exploring the nuances of leading, inspiring, and transforming global and distributed teams. Now, as we pause at the culmination of this exploration, it's time to reflect on the insights gleaned and the path that lies ahead.

Recap of Key Takeaways and Insights from the Book: "Digital Triumph" has unfurled a roadmap for navigating the complexities of digital leadership, illuminating the strategies that bridge the gap between aspiration and achievement in the remote work landscape. We've delved into the heart of digital leadership, unraveling the threads of diversity, technology, and resilience that knit together successful remote teams. From the art of fostering engagement and cohesion across time zones to the mastery of conflict resolution and innovation in a digital context, this volume has offered a compass for entrepreneurs charting their course through the digital age.

Encouraging Ongoing Learning and Adaptation in the

Digital World: The digital frontier is ever-evolving, and mastery in this realm demands an unyielding commitment to continuous learning and adaptation. Embrace the relentless pace of technological advancement as an ally in your quest for leadership excellence. Let curiosity be your guide as you explore new tools, methodologies, and strategies that can enhance your team's productivity and creativity. The journey of digital leadership is one of perpetual evolution—where the willingness to adapt and innovate defines the boundary between the ordinary and the extraordinary.

Empowering Leaders to Inspire and Transform Remote Teams: In the digital expanse, where teams are bound not by geography but by shared visions and goals, the role of the leader transcends traditional boundaries. Arm yourself with the tools of empathy, communication, and cultural intelligence to lead your distributed teams with a global mindset. Recognize that the strength of your leadership is measured not just by the outcomes achieved but by the growth, satisfaction, and resilience of your team members. Embrace the challenge of transforming your remote team into a cohesive, innovative force that thrives on collaboration and diversity.

Embracing Resilience and Fostering a Supportive Network: The digital landscape, with its inherent uncertainties and challenges, tests the mettle of both leaders and teams. Building resilience—both personal and collective—becomes crucial in navigating this terrain. Cultivate an environment where setbacks are viewed as opportunities for learning and growth, and where the support of mentors, peers, and the broader community fuels the journey towards success. It is within this supportive ecosystem that the seeds of resilience germinate, enabling teams to weather the storms of disruption and emerge stronger.

Conclusion: "Digital Triumph" has endeavored to equip you with the insights and strategies to harness the full potential of digital leadership. As you forge ahead, let the principles of innovation, empathy, and continuous learning guide your actions. Remember, the digital world is a canvas of endless potential, waiting for visionary leaders to paint the future with bold strokes of creativity and determination.

In crafting this volume, my journey has been one of discovery and passion—sharing the lessons that have shaped my understanding of digital leadership. It is my fervent hope that "Digital Triumph" serves not just as a guide but as a beacon, illuminating your path to leadership excellence in the digital age.

As we part ways, may your leadership journey be enriched by the diversity, innovation, and resilience that define the digital frontier. May your digital triumph be a testament to the power of visionary leadership in shaping a future where remote teams flourish, creating a legacy that transcends the digital divide.

With heartfelt gratitude, thank you for joining me on this remarkable journey. May your path forward be illuminated by the insights within these pages, guiding you to lead with distinction and inspire a new era of digital triumph.

The Ask

Dear Digital Explorer,

As you reach the end of "Digital Triumph," I hope you find yourself equipped with the insights and strategies needed to navigate the vast and ever-changing digital landscape. If this volume has served as your beacon, guiding you through the intricacies of leading and inspiring remote teams across the digital divide, I warmly invite you to share your journey with a review on Amazon.

Your thoughts, whether they shine with the brilliance of five stars or offer constructive pathways for others to tread, are invaluable. It's through your honest feedback that the essence of "Digital Triumph" becomes a shared treasure, enriching the voyage for fellow entrepreneurs embarking on their digital leadership odyssey.

Eager for more insights and strategies to master the digital realm? Venture further into the "Be A Unicorn" series and other writings by visiting my Amazon author's page (https://www.amazon.com/author/patrickhperrine). Let's continue to forge a community of visionary leaders, each review and shared experience inspiring a new wave of digital triumphs.

Forward into the Future,
    Patrick

About the Author

Patrick H. Perrine is a trailblazing author, mentor, and seasoned entrepreneur with a spirit that exemplifies the essence of entrepreneurship. From his humble beginnings as a paperboy in Minnesota to his emergence as a globally recognized industry leader, his journey epitomizes resilience and determination.

Fueled by an insatiable thirst for knowledge, Patrick opted for university over his senior high school year, setting the stage for his relentless pursuit of personal growth. His tenure with UpStart, an organization championing educational opportunities for first-generation Americans, ignited his lifelong commitment to empowering others, extending beyond business and into his early philanthropic endeavors.

In his twenties, Patrick served as a Founding Board member for The Point Foundation, the largest LGBTQ scholarship foundation today. His dedication to fostering inclusivity and aiding LGBTQ students in higher education continues to positively impact hundreds of lives.

Patrick's entrepreneurial journey took flight with myPartner.com, an online dating service that addressed a critical gap in the market. Recognized as one of the "Best Matchmakers" and "Most Innovative Online Dating Sites" by the iDate Industry, the venture earned a Certificate of Recognition issued by California Legislature Assemblyman Mark Leno. This marked Patrick's first step in a journey filled with identifying unique opportunities and delivering transformative solutions across industries from skincare to dog tech.

Despite the hurdles encountered, Patrick's determination only amplified. His passion for nurturing startups led him to establish Rincon Hill Advisors. During this period, he served as a Steering Committee member for StartOut, a leading nonprofit fostering queer entrepreneurship, and consulted with Fortune 500 companies like Berkshire Hathaway and Intuit.

Adding to his achievements as an entrepreneur, Patrick became an angel investor. His foresight led him to invest in promising startups like MisterB&B, the world's largest gay hotelier, and Roadster, the leading commerce platform for car buying. His dog tech venture, too, gained recognition, leading to his selection as a NGLCC Pitch Finalist and participant in the Seamless IoT Accelerator, earning a $100,000 investment offer as a program graduate.

Most recently, Patrick served as an Entrepreneur in Residence (EiR) with 500 StartUps, an organization committed to uplifting global economies through entrepreneurship. This role solidified his dedication to guiding and uplifting aspiring entrepreneurs.

With a total of six books to his credit, including recent works "Fail Fast, Recover Faster", "Ignite your Dream", and "Fueling the Fire", Patrick continues to share his journey and insights.

His writing reflects his unwavering commitment to guiding entrepreneurs through their unique journeys.

Patrick H. Perrine is more than a summary of his accomplishments. He stands as a testament to the power of determination, innovation, and a generous spirit. His contributions have been acknowledged in global press publications such as Forbes, Advocate, and Mirror, but his most profound impact lies in the lives of the entrepreneurs he's guided, inspired, and empowered.

Subscribe to my newsletter:

✉ https://www.patrickperrine.com

Also by Patrick H. Perrine

Your next adventure in entrepreneurship awaits! Choose your guidebook on Amazon (https://www.amazon.com/author/patrickhperrine) or **www.PatrickPerrine.com/books**, and ignite the spark that takes your venture to new heights. The future is yours to shape!

Unicorn Rising: Ascending to the Pinnacle of Entrepreneurship and the Billionaire's Club

Fueled by entrepreneurial dreams and the allure of the Unicorn Club? Patrick H. Perrine is your guide, offering an unparalleled roadmap set to be every entrepreneur's playbook.

"Unicorn Rising" emerges as the cornerstone of the *Be A Unicorn* series, laying the groundwork that "Digital Triumph" and the other nine volumes build upon.

"Unicorn Rising" is more than a path to towering valuations; it's a compass to innovation, transformative leadership, and sustainable triumph. Dive into leadership's intricacies, the pulse of emerging tech, financial stewardship, and the essence of high-impact entrepreneurship.

However, this isn't a one-size-fits-all roadmap. While Patrick offers foundational wisdom and actionable tools, he accentuates the bespoke nature of each startup's odyssey. Whether you're an entrepreneurial novice or a battle-hardened veteran seeking to recalibrate strategies, this series becomes your beacon.

Embark, defy conventions, and with "Unicorn Rising", elevate to unparalleled entrepreneurial echelons.

Ignite Your Dream: The Quintessential Checklist for Aspiring Entrepreneurs

Ignite Your Dream: The Quintessential Checklist for Aspiring Entrepreneurs" by Patrick H. Perrine is an immersive guide lighting the path towards entrepreneurial success. This power-packed handbook propels you from dreaming to achieving with a carefully curated 100-step map. Dive into real-life entrepreneur stories, extract wisdom, and utilize actionable checklists.

This book transcends theoretical guidelines, providing a mentorship experience designed to turn dreams into reality. Ready to kindle your entrepreneurial spirit? "Ignite your Dream" is your step forward towards unlocking potential and achieving success in the exciting world of entrepreneurship.

Fail Fast, Recover Faster: Bouncing Back From Entrepreneurial Failure

Embrace failure and bounce back stronger with "Fail Fast, Recover Faster: Bouncing Back From Entrepreneurial Failure". It's your guidebook through the tumultuous journey of entrepreneurship, celebrating stumbles as stepping stones towards success. Dive into compelling tales of triumphant entrepreneurs, learn how to pivot rapidly, manage fallout, and convert setbacks into launchpads.

Discover strategies for repairing financial, relationship, and reputation damage, and see your failures as badges of resilience. This transformative book readies you to rebound from failure swiftly, turning your setbacks into your next entrepreneurial triumph. With "Fail Fast, Recover Faster", you're poised to harness your own unicorn moment and turn failure into a launching pad for success.

Fueling the Fire: Nurturing Resilience and Preventing Burnout in Entrepreneurship

In "Fueling the Fire: Nurturing Resilience and Preventing Burnout in Entrepreneurship," seasoned entrepreneur Patrick H. Perrine guides you through the entrepreneurial journey, sharing practical strategies for maintaining resilience and passion. Drawing from 20 years of startup experience, Perrine covers everything from ideation to acquisition.

Discover how to build a support system, manage your time effectively, cultivate a positive work culture, and align your work with your values. Whether you're an experienced entrepreneur or just beginning, "Fueling the Fire" is a must-read for maintaining balance and fulfillment in the dynamic world of entrepreneurship.